chefs in the MARKET

FRESH TASTES AND FLAVOURS FROM GRANVILLE ISLAND PUBLIC MARKET

BILL JONES AND STEPHEN WONG

PHOTOGRAPHS BY DAVID COOPER

RAINCOAST BOOKS
Vancouver

First published in 2000 by

Raincoast Books
8680 Cambie Street
Vancouver, B.C. V6P 6M9
(604) 323-7100
www.raincoast.com

Design by Hermani & Sorrentino Design
Photographs by David Cooper

1 2 3 4 5 6 7 8 9 10

CANADIAN CATALOGUING IN PUBLICATION DATA

Jones, W. A. (William Allen), 1959–
Chefs in the market

Includes index.

ISBN 1-55192-294-0

1. Cookery, Canadian—British Columbia style. 2. Cookery—British Columbia.
3. Granville Island (Vancouver, B.C.) I. Wong, Stephen, 1955– II. Title

TX715.6.J67 2000 641.59711'33 C00-910308-2

Raincoast Books gratefully acknowledges the support of the Government of Canada, through the Book Publishing Industry Development Program, the Canada Council for the Arts and the Department of Canadian Heritage. We also acknowledge the assistance of the Province of British Columbia, through the British Columbia Arts Council.

Printed in Canada

To my wife, Lynn, for putting up with the long, late hours and occasional cranky behaviour. —Bill

To Nina, Christopher and Brielle. —Stephen

contents

ACKNOWLEDGEMENTS

The publication of this book and the success of the *Chefs in the Market* series at Granville Island Public Market are the results of tireless efforts by a host of very special people and good friends. Their names, if listed in full, would probably fill many pages. To all of them, we dedicate this project. It is our hope that this book will serve as a lasting memento of the cherished relationships we've forged along the way and as a token of appreciation to everyone who contributed to it.

Let us begin by expressing our sincere thanks to the management of both the Canada Mortgage and Housing Corporation and the Public Market for their ongoing commitment in support of Chefs in the Market, the program and the book. Special kudos go to Colleen Welsh, the Market's manager, for having faith in us, for sharing in our vision and for her meticulous attention to detail. We also have the Market coordinators, Johanna Hastings, Mary O'Donovan, Patricia Morris and Felix Kaufhold and their staff to thank for their constructive input and their hard work behind the scenes.

In the past three years, many prominent local chefs have taken time out of their busy schedules to share their knowledge and expertise with Market patrons. They were the stars of the show, our teachers and our inspiration. We are especially thankful to them for supplying us with a terrific collection of their recipes and for permitting us to share them in print. Unfortunately, because of space limitations in this book we are unable to include all of the recipes submitted and to pay just tribute to every one of our guest chefs. For that, we apologize.

In addition, we thank the many Market merchants and producers whose excellent products formed the basis for each of our programs. One of our goals was to showcase the natural resources of our region, which include all the great people who pour talent and love into the food they produce. Our work strives to educate the public on the importance of supporting our local farmers and food crafters. They need and deserve all the help and support we can give them.

Our heartfelt gratitude also goes to our dear friends in the media for their kind words and support in publicizing the events and schedules and to our audience, whose enthusiasm and encouragement helped to turn *Chefs in the Market* from an idea into a celebration.

Credit for publication of the book goes to the talented team at Raincoast Books, led by Kevin Williams, which includes Carol Watterson and Brian Scrivener, for the initial shaping of the project; Hermani & Sorrentino Design for the elegant design; Ruth Wilson for recipe editing; and Simone Doust for taking care of the myriad details involved in a project like this. For many of the beautiful photographs of the Market, we thank the talented David Cooper and his team.

Last but not least, we thank Gerry Hill and Chris Hayes from BC Gas for providing us with the cooking stages and cooktops, without which we would have been very much in the cold.

PUBLIC

RKET
NEON PRODUCTS LTD.

INTRODUCTION

The *Chefs in the Market* Experience

It's 7:30 Sunday morning. Granville Island Public Market will not be officially open until 9:00 a.m., but the place is already bustling with activity both inside and out.

On Johnston Street, just beyond the emblematic green, blue and white striped awnings shading the Market's main southerly doors, delivery trucks are jostling for position to unload their cargo. Cartons of meats, totes of fish and crates of fruits and vegetables are hauled off and carted to storage coolers to await processing.

Inside, the butchers, fishmongers and produce sellers are hard at work. Neatly trimmed steaks and chops and fat links of sausages are stacked onto parchment-lined trays inside banks of gleaming glass cases. Yards of open steel bins are filled with crushed ice interlaced with plump, bright-eyed salmon and trout, alongside heaps of oysters, clams and mussels. Boxes of carrots, lettuce, peppers and fruit are inspected, then piled into tidy mounds atop a maze of stilted racks. Meanwhile, the bakers at the various bakeries, who have been busy at their ovens since well before first light, are laying out the first batches of their labour of love. The toasty fragrance of freshly baked breads and the sweet, buttery aroma of cakes and scones, mingled with the heady scent of just-brewed coffee, waft through the Market in intoxicating waves.

By 8:30 the aisles are filling up. Many market-savvy regulars have already caught up on their dose of the weekend's news over a steaming mug and a warm muffin and are now weaving their way through the stalls and produce stands, contemplating what to cook for Sunday dinner.

Under the now familiar yellow banner that marks the spot for our cooking corner, we are picking up our pace in preparation for today's *Chefs in the Market* show. The tables flanking our portable stovetop have to be skirted and decorated. Recipe cards have to be set out for the audience to collect. Then it'll be time to go foraging for ingredients to feature in our first "Market Show & Tell" session, which begins at 11:00 a.m. Being food lovers, we find doing the shopping and conducting these improvisational product education seminars great fun and a challenge. The shopping is the challenging part. We are like kids let loose in a candy store; selecting just a handful of ingredients out of the constant stream of new products being brought to market in the regular stores and from day vendors to present in the show is often tougher that you'd think. Luckily, by staying focused on the changing seasons and our theme for the day, we always manage to pick something fitting and interesting. After that, creating a dish à la minute with the chosen ingredients is a cinch by comparison. In fact, that is the point of the "show and tell" segments – to show how easy and pleasurable it is to try new things.

Before we know it, it's noon. The first of our two guest chefs for the day has arrived and is busy laying out food he's prepared, getting ready to demonstrate the recipe he has created just for this occasion. During this informal cooking class, we are hosts, assistants and, more often than not, eager students. As he cooks, we chat with him about his background and his restaurant. We query him for any cooking tips he may care to share. We field questions from the audience. And we help prepare samples for those gathered around to watch and taste. At 1:00 p.m. our second guest arrives with her sous-chef in tow . . . and on we go with the show.

At 4:00 p.m., when we pack up after another exhilarating day of cooking with *Chefs in the Market*, we will reflect with relish on the new friends we've made and the joy we all shared in one of the simplest yet most satisfying pleasures in life – good food.

How It All Came Together

As food professionals, we have been devoted shoppers at the Public Market for years. It's always our first stop when we're looking for the best products to work with for recipe development, function catering or if we're just entertaining at home. During our frequent forays, early in the morning or mid-afternoon, we have encountered many of the city's culinary notables (sometimes even clad in their chefs' whites) sauntering through the Market, basket in hand, pinching, sniffing, asking questions, hunting for just the right ingredients with which to work their magic. Often, other shoppers recognized them for who they were and asked them for recommendations and cooking tips. So, three years ago, when we were asked to organize a program to promote further awareness of Market produce and merchants, we jumped at the chance. Within weeks, *Chefs in the Market* was developed and launched as a series of cooking shows performed in the heart of the Market, showcasing professional chefs and the wealth of great Market ingredients.

From the start, we saw our program as a great opportunity to bring some of Vancouver's best chefs face-to-face with the public in a friendly, interactive setting. Most chefs, while they may be the driving force behind a successful restaurant, get their feedback secondhand, through their serving staff. Some are shy and are content with this, but most of those we know enjoy communing with their public. It was our intent during these shows to provide a forum for our guest chefs to express their inspiration in full, while allowing the audience to benefit from the demonstration of their techniques and their years of experience. As the popularity of the program grew steadily, we were happy to see that our vision was shared with enthusiasm by both the chefs who participated and the Market audience, many of whom are now on a first-name basis with us.

In general, there are two types of *Chefs in the Market* programs, differing chiefly in size. "Regular" events are located inside the Market, during which two chefs are showcased in sessions interspersed with "Market Show & Tell" segments. Larger programs, featuring up to five chefs, are often part of a "Festival" event held in the north courtyard of the Market under a marquee tent. These are usually combined with entertainment, educational displays and even competitions and games in which the public is invited to participate. Each *Chefs in the Market* program typically revolves around a theme, which may be a seasonal ingredient, such as asparagus in spring; a calendar holiday, such as Thanksgiving; or a style of cooking, such as "The Art of Sushi." For all sessions the chefs are requested to submit their recipes to us prior to the event, and recipe cards are printed for distribution to the audience.

Throughout the years, as you can imagine, we have collected quite a few recipes from the program, all of which are delicious illustrations of how to make the most of the fabulous array of ingredients available in the Market. Equally important is our realization that these recipes are representative of the cooking styles of our contributing chefs – each of them capturing and reflecting a grain of their creative essence. Together, as a collection, they paint a vivid picture of what's been cooking in Vancouver in recent years and envisage what is to come. That's one of the reasons we decided to compile the best of them in this book. We are also unabashedly proud of the role of the Market in our community and want to share the Market experience with a wider audience. To put the icing on the cake, we've gathered recipes and produce tips from the excellent Market merchants, several of whom turned out to be terrific chefs in their own right. We believe we've created a wonderful book for the total enjoyment of the Market experience and a wealth of recipes fit for all occasions. As chefs, we know the proof is in the pudding, and we hope you will enjoy our tribute to a unique market and learn to treasure Granville Island Public Market as the jewel in the crown of Vancouver.

A Day at the Market—Stephen Wong

Whether it's a dewy spring morning, a scorching summer afternoon, a golden Indian-summer day in fall or a darkening wintry eve, a trip to Granville Island Public Market is always a delight. It's a welcome distraction from hectic concerns, a chance to recharge. In fact, going for coffee at the Market has become a regular part of our family's entertainment. In recent years we're likely to be there two or three times a week, as my daughter attends dance classes at the nearby Arts Umbrella studios.

Our ritual almost always begins with a *caffee latte* and a shared snack: a raspberry scone or a piece of bumbleberry pie with ice cream, a taco salad or some piroshkis, or just a heart-warming bowl of soup. I've learned from experience that it's important to fortify myself before going shopping. It's the only way to keep my binge buying impulses from running amok.

After catching up on the family's news or taking in a performance by a talented busker, it's time to tour the stalls and shops and think about dinner. Careful consideration is needed. It's less a process of choosing what to buy than a prudent, resolute resistance of temptation. Mounds of carefully stacked berries, bins of gleaming tomatoes, bundles of asparagus, rows of steaks, roasts and sausages, ice-binfuls of shiny salmon, trays of onyx-hued scallops, live lobsters and crabs scuttling in chilled tanks, buckets of spiced olives, heaps of pastas, beckoning wedges of cheese – not to mention the persistent wafting scent of freshly baked breads. I can feel my resolve weakening.

It's time to consult the experts, the merchants whom I've grown to know quite well through the years. Knowing my preference for what's local and fresh, they are often my resident menu planners. In fact, getting to know the vendors and being confident that they know their products and know what I like are all reasons why I shop at the Market. I know I'll get the best in quality, delivered with a generous helping of good cheer. At the end of a busy day, sometimes that's as nourishing as a good meal.

In the summer months, I always take time to visit the farmers who come to sell their produce directly from the back of their trucks in the Arts Club Theatre parking lot next door. Organic heritage tomatoes bursting with flavour, picked that morning in the Okanagan, thumb-sized new nugget potatoes trucked from Pemberton – all planted, nurtured and delivered with a passion that reassures me that my food and the land from which it's grown are in good hands.

Of course, not every Market visit can be as leisurely. Sometimes, getting something quick and easy to sate the family's appetite is paramount. That's when you'll see me dashing through the Market, grabbing a few marinated chicken kebabs from Armando's, a handful of mesclun salad from Four Seasons Farm, some penne pasta and a bag of grated Parmesan from Zara's, and a bottle of house-made dressing from the Stock Market. Ten minutes at the Market and 20 minutes at home and dinner's on the table. Phew!

Although I don't live really nearby, Granville Island has become a big part of my life. Looking in my photo albums the other day, I realized that the Market, in its seasonal glory – bright and colourful in summer, quiet and white with snow one particular winter – has been the backdrop in snapshots of my children since they were toddlers. My oldest is now 19 and we're still meeting "for coffee" at the Market.

Seasonal Delights of the Market—Bill Jones

Eating according to the season used to be a traditional necessity. We feasted on the bounty of the warm months and we subsisted on our stored larder in the bleak winter months. With each shift of the seasons we revelled in the ebb and flow of anticipation and excitement for what was next to come. Somewhere in our evolution, things changed. Now, underripe and bland-tasting produce from all corners of the Earth is available to us year-round, and we have become jaded, far too willing to accept the trade-off of supplanting flavour with variety and supply. Thankfully, not everyone is buying into the convenience and seduction of the seasonless global economy. Caring growers are rediscovering the heritage foods of our ancestors, and enlightened shoppers are looking for ways to eat seasonal produce and support the efforts of our local agricultural community. To illustrate the joy of seasonal eating, let's take a stroll through our local calendar.

Spring arrives in Vancouver with a burst of daffodils and crocuses. While the North Shore mountains are still crusted in snow, farmers who have nurtured their delicate crops through the mild winter are now delivering the first local young greens to grace our salad bowls. Soon, tender stalks of asparagus will arrive in the Market. Following the lead of the spring morels, the trickle of the harvest grows into a flood. Stinging nettle, rhubarb, mustard greens and fiddleheads arrive, and before we know it local strawberries are filling the tables – crimson, juicy, sweet-tart berries that have a depth of flavour unmatched by the bloated bulk of imports from the south.

By now, **summer** is thundering at our door. Soon, cherries will be piled high in boxes all through the market, trucked in from the Okanagan, cool, purplish red, plump and hefty with lip-staining juice. Bing and Van cherries are the most common varieties, but the best is yet to come. I've been waiting all year long for the Rainier cherries to arrive. A local specialty, Rainiers are golden orbs that are lightly brushed with pink. Their yellow flesh, sweeter than any other cherry, is a source of pure joy to me. Local farmers set up day tables in the aisles of the market; baby beets, still clinging to their soil, lie next to full heads of crisp lettuce. The bounty is upon us.

The shortening of the days heralds the return of **fall**, my favourite season. The crispness in the evening air, the changing colours of leaves and the scent of ripe McIntosh apples are all triggers of tender memories from a youth spent running through fields and orchards. As I grew older, autumn became a fascination for another reason – wild mushrooms. I am continually thrilled to see new varieties of wild mushrooms for sale in the Market, piled near tables of colourful squash, ears of sweet, juicy corn and crates of just-picked apples. At this time of year, it's hard to leave the Market without several groaning bags of produce.

Once the delicate trees have dropped their leaves, the rains come with a saturating regularity and local produce slows to a trickle. **Winter** has arrived with horizontal rains and erratic weather patterns. At this time of year you have to be really creative to feast on the best of local produce. Thankfully, greenhouse technology has yielded tomatoes, cucumbers and peppers to spice up our diets. I personally crave green cabbage sautéed with garlic or ginger. It seems to fit every occasion as a side dish to any starch or protein. Often, I take solace in the bins of dry goods brimming with preserved products, new grains to experiment with, dried nuts and fruits to jazz up rice and polenta dishes. I try not to be too regimented in my lust for local goods; besides, the tropical fruits are far too appealing. Try to think of the winter as a time for harmless flirtation, and when spring rolls around again, you'll be renewing those vows of true love.

Local Seasonal Products

Early Spring	June	July	August	Fall & Winter
Arugula	Asian vegetables	Apricots	Apples	Artichokes
Asian greens	Asparagus	Basil	Beets	Brussels sprouts
Chives	Cauliflower	Blueberries	Blackberries	Chanterelles
Fiddlehead ferns	Cherries	Broccoli	Celery	Crabapples
Garlic shoots	Green onions	Cabbage	Corn	Cranberries
Morel mushrooms	Lavender	Carrots	Currants	Figs
Mustard greens	Lettuce	Cucumbers	Eggplant	Grapes
Parsley	Marjoram	Dill	Gooseberries	Hazelnuts
Pea tips	New potatoes	Garlic	Kale	Kiwi fruit
Radishes	Rosemary	Green beans	Long beans	Leeks
Spinach	Sage	Loganberries	Melons	Onions
Spring greens	Salad greens	Nectarines	Pears	Parsnips
Stinging nettles	Strawberries	Peaches	Plums	Pine mushrooms
Watercress	Sweet peas	Peppers	Shallots	Pumpkins
	Tarragon	Raspberries	Swiss chard	Quince
	Thyme	Zucchini	Tomatillos	Truffles
			Tomatoes	Turnips
				Walnuts
				Winter squash

Year-Round BC-Grown Products

Greenhouse products: tomatoes, peppers, cucumbers, herbs, lettuce, salad greens
Mushrooms: white button, brown button (cremini), portobello, oyster, shiitake, enoki
Fish: wild and farmed salmon, halibut, green cod, snapper, albacore tuna, rockfish, Pacific sole, trout, Arctic char, etc.
Seafood: clams, mussels, oysters, scallops, geoduck
Crustaceans & Cephalopods: Dungeness crab, spot prawns, squid, octopus
Cheese: Cheddar, goat, blue, Edam, Gouda, mozzarella, bocconcini, etc.
Dairy: milk, yogourt, sour cream, goat's milk, buttermilk, etc.
Eggs: chicken, duck, quail
Meats: beef, pork, lamb, goat
Game: venison, wild boar, muskox, rabbit, wild turkey, etc.
Poultry: chicken, turkey, duck, goose, quail, Cornish hen, guinea fowl, ostrich, emu, etc.
Grains: peas, beans, lentils, chickpeas, etc.
Nuts: hazelnuts, walnuts

GRANVILLE ISLA

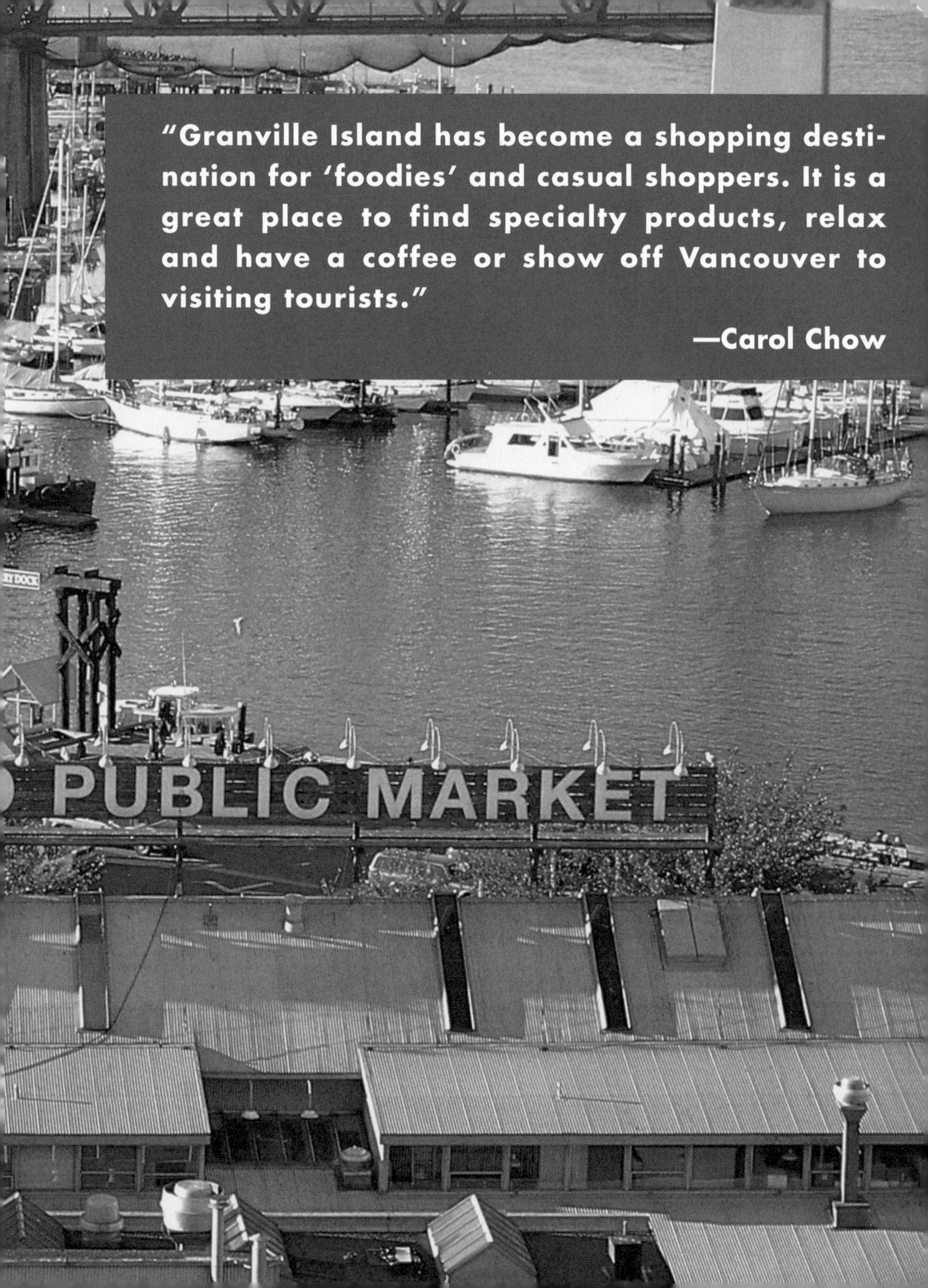

"Granville Island has become a shopping destination for 'foodies' and casual shoppers. It is a great place to find specialty products, relax and have a coffee or show off Vancouver to visiting tourists."

—Carol Chow

Granville Island—A Brief History

Early History: Before humans arrived on the scene, the region was covered in ancient old-growth forests of mammoth Sitka spruce and Douglas fir. The site of present-day Granville Island was a rich intertidal zone teeming with life. Large sandbars and beaches were the main topography. Local creeks boiled with salmon returning to spawn. A rich Native culture eventually emerged, and the "island" became a favourite spot to erect fish weirs designed to trap a share of the fat salmon headed upstream. Villages sprung up nearby, carved into the heavily wooded landscape. When the Europeans arrived, roughly 5,000 years later, they set into motion a series of events that would rapidly transform the area.

The Pioneering Late 1800s: The area was developed into a small mill town called Granville, and a bridge was built to span False Creek. The bridge's foundation, reinforced by piles driven into the sandbars, eventually caught the eye of enterprising parties and talk of creating usable land from the tidal flats began.

Early 1900s: Almost a million cubic yards of fill dredged from False Creek was used to reclaim 35 acres of land, initially dubbed Industrial Island. Industries sprang up to supply the burgeoning lumber, mining and shipping enterprises of the day. The harbourfront on one side and the railway at the back provided excellent access. Iron was forged into bridges, machinery and nails; paint and barrels were also manufactured in a beehive of activity.

The 1950s: Some of the Island's biggest customers had outgrown the area and, with their relocation, the hum of the Island fell almost silent. A few light industries soldiered on, but by and large, the Island had become a fire hazard and an ecological liability, surrounded by a waterway choked with pollution.

The 1960s: Vancouver was an enterprising place in the era of love and social revolution. The city contained many vibrant communities, and a concept for redesigning the industrial landscape of the Island into a public space for all to enjoy evolved. Ideas started to emerge to take advantage of the infrastructure of industry and rejuvenate it into a plan of mixed residential, park and commercial development.

The 1970s: The industrial buildings were cleaned up and renovated to house markets, restaurants, a hotel, artisans' studios, boat builders and the renowned Emily Carr Institute of Art and Design. One of the largest buildings was gutted and retrofitted into the bustling

Public Market, where the freshest produce would be available, even on a Sunday. The Island was purposely developed as a place where commerce and the arts would freely mix. Facilities were built to house the many theatre, performance art and entertainment venues, and to proudly display local talent.

Today: Granville Island, anchored by the Public Market, one of North America's most successful and popular public markets, boasts eight million visits annually. Locals come down to the Island and bring their visitors to show it off because its location captures the essential beauty of the city. The plazalike atmosphere exudes a unique sense of community and celebration, making it an ideal meeting place for area residents and visitors alike.

The Public Market—Quality, Service and Diversity

Since its inception, planners knew that the Public Market, being the anchor of Granville Island, had to offer the best in both quality products and service. To achieve this, great pains have been taken to ensure that the mix of merchants is comprehensive. Merchants are chosen for their expertise in their field of food, their ability to communicate about their products and their commitment to provide superior personal service to their customers. Twenty-one merchants were hand-picked for the opening in 1979, and that number has increased throughout the years to about 50.

In addition to the permanent stores with long-term leases, planners and management have also reserved space in the Market for up to 50 day vendors. This provision has ensured a continual turnover of farmers, producers and craftspeople in tune with the changing seasons.

In recent years, in support of local farmers who have to travel from outside the Lower Mainland, a Farmers Truck Market has been added. Every Thursday from May to October, growers from as far as the Okanagan Valley or Pemberton congregate in the parking lot adjacent to the Market to sell their produce from the backs of their vehicles. For those in the know, just-picked heirloom tomatoes, field sweet corn, new nugget potatoes, juicy peppers and a cornucopia of succulent vine- and tree-ripened fruits are among the treasure trove of offerings.

This strategy of blending consistent quality with ever-changing diversity has proven to be the key to the ongoing success of the Market. Customers are not only assured of excellent quality, they can also find something new with every visit. The dynamic marketplace is a prime reason why many of the best chefs in the city are regular customers. Many have developed long-term supplier relationships with both merchants and farmers.

Another factor contributing to the success of the Market is its commitment to consumer education. Customers are encouraged to ask questions about the foods they buy. While doing so, they are prompted to expand their scope and interest in food. In turn this becomes the incentive for the merchants to seek out an ever-expanding array of products to satiate the increasingly informed and curious customer. The *Chefs in the Market* series is one program that is the direct result of this commitment.

Shopping at the Market—A Virtual Tour

The best way to shop at Granville Island Public Market is to go with an open heart and a spirit of adventure. If you have a recipe in mind, bring the list along to make your trip productive. If you are looking for inspiration, simply walk around the Market and let your senses be your guide. If you don't know what something is, or how to cook it, ask the merchants. If you are looking for an unusual item or have a special request, again feel free to ask. If the merchant doesn't have it, chances are he or she will either find it for you or guide you to a suitable alternative. As any of the chefs in this book will tell you, good cooking starts with good ingredients. Getting good ingredients means finding a reliable merchant with a strong sense of pride in the business. The Market is filled with such merchants, so take some time to get to know your Market and when in doubt, ask. That's what the chefs do.

Of course, the Market experience is by no means only about shopping for food. It's also about atmosphere. It's about taking a little time to gaze at the myriad watercrafts that float by on False Creek or grabbing a snack and a moment of respite from a hectic day while listening to a busker playing his guitar. It's about chuckling at your children chasing the pigeons in the courtyard and sharing in their glee. It's really about appreciating life in Vancouver.

So come along. Let's take an armchair tour and see what we might find . . .

Seafood

For years now, the Granville Island Public Market has been well known as one of Vancouver's most consistent sources for the best fish and seafood, and we have a trio of Market fish stores to thank for that. While they all carry staple items such as salmon and halibut fillets, tiger prawns and bay scallops, they do differ somewhat in focus and approach. Janice Kariotakis, ever ready with a smile and a kindly greeting, runs the immaculate **Salmon Shop**, which is long on the variety of products they stock and excels at providing efficient and friendly service. Octopus, marlin, a line of Russian caviar and a handful of ready-to-cook marinated fish are among some of the unique products found here. At the west end of the market, you'll find the excellent **Longliner Seafoods**. The owners, Jim and Dave Moorehead, were formerly salmon fishers, so if you're looking for fresh, frozen or smoked wild B.C. salmon, you've come to the right place. Other value-added products encased in glass include an excellent naturally smoked sablefish, smoked and pepper mackerel fillets, Sweden matjes herring fillets, Nyborg herring fillets and Indian candy (smoked salmon). In the east corner of the market, Takashi Hamataki, owner of **Seafood City**, has taken crustacean and mollusk freshness to a new height. Here, Dungeness crabs, lobsters, clams, mussels and oysters are routinely kept in live tanks. Occasionally, live local spot prawns are available, too. It's also no surprise that sushi-grade ahi tuna, sea urchin roe and whole fishes such as carp, sea bass and snapper are prominent on his ice trays, alongside a full range of sushi supplies.

Meat and Poultry

Another key Public Market food shopping experience is being able to get up close and personal with a good butcher. Imagine you've found a delicious recipe for pork crown roast that you dearly want to serve as the centrepiece for your special dinner party, but the butchering instructions have left you cold. Armando Bacani of **Armando's Finest Quality Meats** is one man you might want to see. He'll help you pick out the cut of meat that's best suited for the task, dress it, truss it and have it ready for you to pick up. Check out his fine display of marinated products to make your next meal a quick and painless process.

Another butcher who boasts a long tenure in the Market is Adolf Henneberger (if he's not around, ask for Mike or Erwin) of **Tenderland Meats**, justly famous for his excellent sausages. Adolf is particularly proud of the lamb sausages. Flavoured with mint, they are juicy and meaty, perfect for a summer barbecue or a winter stew. Eight other varieties are in stock, alongside double-smoked bacon, marinated pork chops, spiced back ribs and a host of other ready-to-use items. If you are in a hurry to put dinner on the table, both of the butchers will have a vast array of choices for you. Special cuts of well-aged meats are their pride and joy.

If you're looking for free-range and specialty chickens that actually taste like chicken, head over to **Dressed To Go Poultry**. Robert Buller has an eye for good poultry and seeks out the highest quality birds available for his many valued customers. They come back year after year for that special free-range or organic turkey for the holidays. He occasionally carries a wild stock turkey, a smaller bird, weighing 5 to 10 lbs/2 to 5 kg, that will feed four to six people. A line of duck, goose, pheasant, quail, Cornish hen, guinea fowl, ostrich and emu are also available on a regular basis. As the name of the business implies, Robert carries a fine selection of pâtés, sausages and ready-to-eat products such as rosemary-and-lemon-roasted

chicken, plus ready-to-cook products such as Thai-marinated chicken legs and chicken schnitzel. These products make cooking dinner as easy as a turn of the knob on your oven.

Still on the topic of poultry, two merchants are unrivalled in their respective feathered expertise. First, there is Mary Ternes of the **Gran Isle Turkey Stop**. Her shop is utterly and totally concerned with turkey and any products you can imagine that can be made therefrom: sausages, bacon, smokies, pepperoni, garlic rings, roasts, pot pies, cabbage rolls, burgers – not to mention turkeys in whole or in part. There's almost enough variety to have turkey 365 days a year, and if Mary had her way, everyone would be doing just that.

Nathan Kang of **Granville Island Poultryland** is the other poultry purveyor in the Market. Son of Thomas Kang, who started Le Kiu Poultry in Chinatown, Nathan claims to have access to anything that's ever had (or still has) feathers on it. "Just ask, and we'll do our best." So ask, because Nathan also proclaims that serving his customers on the Island is a great joy in his life.

Stocks and Sauces

One of the most helpful stores in the Market has to be Joanne and Georges Lefebvre's **Stock Market**. Judging by the glowing press clippings that line the walls and counters of their store, and the constant queue of customers waiting to be served, Joanne and Georges have good reason to feel bullish about their store. In 1986, having enjoyed considerable success at their small Kitsilano restaurant, Le Chef et Sa Femme, the Lefebvres had a vision. Anticipating increasing interest in good cooking and the household time-crunch that was already beginning to set in, they created their instantly thriving business to "provide Market customers with tasty and healthy shortcuts to gourmet cooking." Through the years, their all-natural, additive-free product line grew steadily to include basic stocks, sauces, marinades, salad dressings, chutneys, compound butters and more. The products are tastefully presented and marked with colourful labels complete with serving suggestions. As we move into the new millennium, look for the appearance of more organic products on their shelves. By the way, they are also famous for their filling hot breakfast cereal – a great way to kick-start your day – and their hearty soups.

Produce

A familiar and enticing sight at the Market for both locals and visitors are the bins of neatly arranged produce and fruit and the precariously and painstakingly stacked pyramid-like baskets of berries. The colourful and mouth-watering displays at produce stands such as **Granville Island Produce, Buddy's Farm, Four Seasons Farm** and **Sunlight Farms** are symbolic of the Market experience. Maintaining eye appeal is only a partial activity of the army of well-trained produce workers who are constantly sorting through fruits, trimming vegetables and replenishing the shelves. The main purpose of their labour is to deliver uncompromised quality to the seasoned Market shoppers who have come to expect the best. The four permanent tenants compete for their share of the business in the Market. Having to keep the competitive edge may well be what keeps the produce quality at such high levels here. The owners seem to keep a close parity of prices, but it always pays to shop and compare to seek out the best deals. But remember, all fruits and vegetables are not created equal. There are varying degrees of quality, and a higher price often yields you a superior product.

What you can't find in the area of fruit or vegetative exotica from the above quartet you might discover at **South China Seas Trading Co.** Focused on the foods of Asia, India, the Caribbean and Latin America, this emporium of exotic tastes stocks spices, flavourings, condiments and uncommon fruits and vegetables. Stacked on the back wall can even be found a representative collection of cookbooks from these regions. In season, there are baskets of wild mushrooms for sale, including rare finds such as pine mushrooms, fresh morels and the fragrant cauliflower fungus. Since 1987 owner Don Dickson and his knowledgeable staff have been dispensing cooking tips and sourcing hard-to-find ingredients for their clientele, which includes some of Vancouver's top chefs.

Now that you are armed with the curry powder you need for your dhal, it's time to find the right lentil. For that you need to go see Nam and Joosun Kim at **The Grainry**. Don't let the compact size of the store discourage you. Step in and you will find custom-tiered fibreglass bins filled with grains, beans, rice, nuts and even a tofu burger mix. Apart from being known for a good selection of dried fruits (some of which are organic and unsulfured), the store also caters to vegans and to customers prone to food allergies.

Italian Specialties

If you are dreaming of Tuscany, a visit to the Market's merchants will take you partway there. At **Duso's Pasta & Cheese**, you'll find Mauro Duso, one of the Market originals and a pioneer who focused on Mediterranean fare long before the Mediterranean diet became *de rigueur* for the health-conscious gourmand. In his packed deli-style store you might find a glossary of Duso's hand-picked dried herbs and spices or, displayed in the antipasto case, roasted peppers, pickled artichokes and more varieties of olives than you can imagine. A nearby basket might contain robust fresh herbs for pestos and sauces next to stacked containers of Parmesan cheese. Olive oils, balsamic vinegars, mustards – all the essentials of the region are lined up on the counters.

At **Zara's Pasta Nest**, John, Luisa and Loris are always in full production. Devoted to freshness, they have chosen to make most of what they sell right at the shop in the Market, from traditional homemade sauces and pestos to fresh pastas. You can watch them while they work. Some popular items here are fresh or marinated bocconcini, custom-imported Italian prosciutto, and handmade tortellini. Sounds like dinner is almost ready.

Baked Goods

What's dinner without a good loaf? At this point in our virtual tour we'll move to the working bakeries in the Market. The best route is to follow your nose. If the yeasty, toasty fragrance of bread baking in the imported French stone-hearth ovens of **Terra Breads** is what attracts the crowds, the toothsome texture and wholesome taste of their naturally leavened sourdough is what keeps them coming back. Or perhaps it's their signature grape focaccia studded with fresh grapes and pine nuts, or those addictive dark-chocolate brownies. Since Terra arrived at the Market, their repertoire has grown steadily under the gentle guidance of owner-chef Mary Mackay. We can hardly wait to see what's next.

Another source of rustic breads, located at the opposite end of the Market, is **Stuart's Bakery**. Here, cakes, pies and a full range of baked goods are among the array of temptations: blackberry mousse, fresh-fruit cream cakes, fruit flans, cheesecakes, a gorgeous-looking organic apple pie, pecan pie, sausage rolls, scones . . . the list goes on.

The Market may open daily at 9:00 a.m., but before first light, at the ovens behind the gleaming glass cases lined with wicker baskets at **Siegel's**, the baker has been turning out dozens of bagels that will eventually end up in children's lunch boxes and on dinner tables. Twenty varieties are available daily, including the ever-popular sesame and poppy seed bagels, a savoury pesto bagel, a sweet banana walnut bagel, a pizza bagel slathered with cheese and tomato sauce and, our all-time favourite, the sweet cream cheese-filled bagel with chewy, flaky dough. For hungry shoppers, 10 different flavoured cream cheeses are on hand ready to be spread onto the bagel of your choice, on the spot. Potato knishes, latkas and matzo crisps are other tasty snacks that are made fresh here everyday.

Dairy Products

If you're looking for fresh cream cheese, excellent yogourt, cholesterol-reduced Born 3 eggs, organic butter or just a scoop of ice cream to brighten your day, visit Morie Ford and Bill McIntosh at **The Milkman**. The store moves a lot of product and insures that the freshest dairy items are available. A wide selection of juice and bottled water is also on hand.

Dussa's Ham & Cheese is a real treasure in the Market. A fixture since the opening of the Market, Arthur Dussa has been educating and cultivating a loyal clientele to the wonderful world of fine cheese. When he retired three years ago, he passed on his legacy to the capable hands of Leslene Schonberger, wife of Werner (a prominent Vancouver wine merchant). Dussa's stocks an outstanding collection of European and regional cheeses, including David Wood's array of wonderful Salt Spring Island goat and sheep cheeses. Ask them about unpasteurized French cheeses such as the exquisite Camembert, one of the world's truly great treats.

Sweet Treats

Since 1979 the sweet smells emanating at 8:00 a.m. from the **Muffin Granny** have been the signal for regulars to come and enjoy a muffin or a "scrumpet" (a sconelike pastry) with their daily java before heading off to work. Muffin selections include oatmeal, apple-cranberry, lemon poppy seed, blueberry, triple berry bran, coffee mocha chocolate chip and low-fat oatmeal raspberry. Those tasty scrumpets are available in blueberry, raspberry, raisin and cheese versions.

While muffins may help fuel an early-morning start, midmorning or afternoon coffee breaks are the definitive realm of donuts. Head to Alan and Betty-Ann's **Lee's Donuts** for the freshest product possible. Step outside the Market door right next to the shop and you can see the bakers working on the next batches right before your eyes. The pillowy soft texture of a fresh doughnut is definitely one of life's treats. Betty-Ann's creativity was tested during our most recent Tomato Festival. When asked to try making something in honour of the tomato, she created a doughnut stuffed with a sweet tomato jam, a surprisingly tasty combination,

If that isn't enough to satisfy your sweet tooth, **Laurelle's Fine Foods** may have just the collection of goodies that will hit the spot: walnut pie, toll house flan, berry crumble, blueberry raspberry almond tart, chocolate-filled kugel or, perhaps, orange-lemon poppy seed cheesecake? It's like having a grandmother hidden away in the Market, baking goodies for her extended family. Savoury fans will not be disappointed, either, as the shop carries a selection of salads, rolls and nibbles that will satisfy the most discriminating palates.

For the ultimate sugar rush, there is no better fix than handcrafted candy. At **Olde World Fudge**, you have a choice of caramel, white- or dark-chocolate almond bark, seafoams, and 12 flavours of fudges, from blueberry to chocolate, all tempered in the meticulously polished copper basin set out at the front corner of the store. They also whip up tempting chocolate-dipped strawberries and caramel apples to trap unsuspecting passersby.

Hard-core chocolate lovers will appreciate the full range of house-made truffles and bonbons offered at **House of Brussels Chocolate**. Hedgehogs, truffles, cream- and liqueur-filled gems are among the customary offerings. For the budget-minded, seconds that are just as tasty are put on sale regularly. But what makes this small shop difficult to walk past, especially if you have kids in tow, are the chocolate-dipped ice cream bars: squares of vanilla ice cream, instantly coated with rich dark-chocolate sauce, then sprinkled with crushed almonds.

For an old-fashioned look at candy, harking back to the legendary five-and-dime stores, drop by to see John or Cara at the **Candy Kitchen**. They have candies for all occasions, not to mention the best collection of PEZ in any neighbourhood. It's funny how this little shop in the middle of the Public Market can feel so remarkably like the ideal corner store of one's childhood dreams.

Beverages

There are many places where you can get a cup of coffee in the Market, but only two deal in the retailing of beans and ground coffee. John Neates Jr., namesake of **JJ Bean – The Coffee Roaster**, is committed to his company's mission statement: "To provide the highest quality fresh roasted beans and memorable customer service to those who love coffee." This belief is the modus operandi that has spelled success for his father, John Sr., who entered the coffee trade more than 20 years ago. Mindful of the Market's tradition of having merchants actually produce some of what they sell on site, staff roast coffee in the small working roaster at the front of the shop. John believes the quality of his coffee speaks for itself. He says, "Come and see for yourself. The proof is in the cup."

Doug Graf and his partner Holly Rodgers are also serious about their coffee, not merely its quality and taste, but also its source. Captured in the name of their shop, **Origins Coffee**, is their goal to sell only "fairly traded" coffee from small producers who practise sustainable, organic agriculture. In doing so they believe they can enhance both the quality of the coffee and the lifestyle and environment of the grower communities while responsibly running their own business. Presently, approximately 90 percent of their coffee is organic. An experienced and skilled roaster, Doug continually experiments with quality beans, blending and refining his craft, searching for the ultimate cup of coffee. Holly, a Fine Arts graduate, is behind the style and élan of the shop that has won over a legion of new fans. The couple also offer a fine selection of premium tea. In the summer, their iced fruit tea is a refreshing way to quench your thirst when the heat is reflecting off the water and warm winds are blowing from the Interior.

Amid the sea of coffee, **Granville Island Tea Company**'s Mark Mercier is convinced that it's time for tea to make a comeback. Mark is a firm believer in the Market traditions of providing personal service and sound product information. His store has been designed to do just that. Surrounded by shelves neatly lined with tea cans is a square counter ringed with stools. Before they buy, customers are invited to sit down and taste some of the more than 75 "base teas," hand-selected and imported by Mark from the world's prominent tea producing regions. Novices and enthusiasts alike are encouraged to create their own favourite blend from the stock: "Our mission is to help people to find their own favourite blend of tea."

When the Market opened, the **Okanagan Wine Shops** set a precedent by being the first privately owned store to sell wine in British Columbia. Since then it's become a convenient spot to pick up some of the select VQA wines produced in the province. Kathleen Ross, who manages the store, is well known in the business for her interest and knowledge in the art of pairing food and wine. If in doubt, drop by and have a chat with her or one of her knowledgeable staff. This shop also carries a great selection of gift bags and other wine paraphernalia that would make nice stocking stuffers for that special wine buff in your life.

Other Services

Apart from food and beverage vendors, Granville Island also has two full-service flower shops. If you're looking for a show-stopping flower arrangement, Linda and Suzanne Hong of **Granville Island Florist** are the resident experts. In fact, the variety of cut flowers and exotic flora that they stock is striking, considering the space of their shop. The **V & J Plant Shop**, in addition to a colourful stock of flowers, seems to have an edge when it comes to dried flowers, potted plants and display pieces such as hanging boxes and planters. For flowers to adorn the table or to charm a loved one, the Public Market has the goods.

The newest addition to the Market, **Gaia Garden Herbal Dispensary**, specializes in herbal medicine and aromatherapy. They offer over 100 organic, wild-crafted dried herbs and herb tea blends for health and pleasure. Herbal tinctures, essential oils, syrups, liniments, ointments and creams are among their stock.

For those who have a little time to linger in the Market and wish for some interesting reading material, **The Smoke Shop** carries a good selection of popular magazines, local newspapers and imports such as the *Wall Street Journal* and the *New York Times*.

Market Dining

For families, the Public Market is much more than a place for food shopping; it's also a place where everyone can find something they like to eat. The Food Court at the Market was originally confined to the west end of the building but, by popular demand, it has since spilled over to the north side of the east wing. Here's a glimpse of what is currently offered.

A La Mode's trademark neon sign, a red circle wedged by twin radiant blue lines, has become a beacon for pie-lovers in Vancouver. More than a dozen tender-crusted classics are available daily. For those whose taste tends to the savoury, there is the chunky chicken pot pie, a hearty beef stew pot pie and the quintessentially West Coast salmon pie. But for sweet-tooths of all ages, the hand-high lemon meringue, the full-bodied bumbleberry and the rich butter tart are irresistible. A wedge of pie lathered with ice cream, a glass mug of coffee, tea or hot chocolate and a bout of spirited conversation around one of the nearby pine tables constitute a habitual family pastime for many Market-goers.

A chunk of Ukrainian sausage, a handful of varenyky (mini-perogies stuffed with cheddar cheese and mashed potatoes) and a cabbage roll are the kind of heart-warming fare that one needs when taking refuge in the Market on a rainy day. **Babushka's Kitchen** is the place to go for these hearty East European specialties. For a snack, you might want to opt for piroshkis – picture-perfect bread rolls baked to a golden turn with a choice of fillings: cheese and potato, broccoli, spinach and potato, and sweet onions and potato or lean ground beef.

Where in Vancouver can you find a window table with an unobstructed harbour view, read your paper, sip your coffee and while away the hour all for the price of a cup of coffee? The answer, known to the legion who frequent the Market for a little respite from their hectic daily routines or just to reaffirm the fact that they live in one of the most spectacular cities in the world, is the **Blue Parrot Espresso Bar**. This glass-lined room with a view and an open attic offers good quality sandwiches, pastries and a full complement of beverages from a self-serve counter, where a lineup is everpresent but always briskly and cheerfully served.

A market by the sea simply would not be complete without a shop that sells fish and chips. At **Celine's Fish & Chips**, there's cod, halibut and salmon, with the obligatory chips. But there are also fried oysters, prawns and squid. They also offer Vietnamese hot and sour seafood soup, halibut rice chowder, clam chowder, shrimp salad, shrimp cocktail, seafood spring rolls and Vietnamese shrimp salad roll. Celine's also has bubble tea, made with tapioca pearls and tropical fruit flavours.

Fred and Judi Glick of **Fraser Valley Juice & Salad Bar** are merchants who have wholeheartedly embraced the Market's commitment to freshness and quality. Ever a pioneer, Judy served fresh orange juice to Market customers before it became available in supermarkets. She also introduced the Vietnamese salad roll to the masses here. In 1985, with Fiona McLeod, Judy co-wrote *The Granville Island Cookbook*, still for sale at Blackberry Books. Their menu today includes banana berry coolers and fresh orange, grapefruit, organic carrot, apple, honeydew, cantaloupe and watermelon juices. There are also bean salads, rice salads, pasta salad, potato salad, classic Caesar and a range of healthful vegetarian stir-fries.

The place in the Market for authentic Chinese fast food is the **Gourmet Wok**, which serves restaurant-quality servings of noodles, fried rice, barbecue duck, sweet-and-sour pork, spareribs in black bean sauce, dumplings and many daily specials.

Sometimes there is nothing as satisfying as a well-made sandwich. For these times, the **Kaisereck Deli** is the right place to make a beeline for. Hot foods such as Polish bratwurst, Bavarian smokies and European wieners are served on a bun. Garnishes include the usual mustard, relish, pickles and onions, and the essential taste of warm sauerkraut. You can order a custom sandwich or have deli meats packed for an impromptu picnic or simply to take home to enjoy.

Succulent Mexican-spiced barbecue chicken and other Latin delicacies await you at **La Tortilleria**. Taco salads, burritos, chimichangas, quesadillas and enchiladas are all prepared with fresh Market ingredients and served with rice, beans and guacamole. For breakfast, huevos rancheros are a zesty way to start the day.

Cal Ostrander and Monty Cooper's **Market Grill** has a solid reputation for serving some of the tastiest and most innovative burgers in town. The deluxe classic comes loaded with lettuce, tomatoes, the usual trimmings and optional toppings of mushrooms, bacon, cheese or sauerkraut. Oozing with cream cheese and guacamole, mushrooms and crisp bacon, their nod to California is the ultimate in sloppy-burger satisfaction. For fish lovers, the Cajun salmon burger is spiked with subtle heat, tempered by sour cream and, like its peers, accompanied by a heap of buffalo fries cut from market-fresh potatoes.

At **Omi of Japan**, Market shoppers continually line up for delicious Japanese hot food. Beef, chicken or pork topped with ginger or teriyaki sauce and served with teppan vegetables are among the most popular items. Dishes are available over excellent short-grained rice or udon noodles – a challenging but tasty thick noodle. Like many of the shop's fans, you might crave the sushi made before your eyes. You can also pick up a premade sushi box (in a variety of styles) for a quick and healthy meal or snack.

For tasty Mediterranean food, **Phoenix Fast Food** carries a wide selection of Greek delicacies: hearty and rustic food such as pita sandwiches, falafel, Greek salad and olive oil–roasted potatoes. An excellent chicken and rice chowder will warm you up on a cool day, while good crispy calamari with tzatziki dipping sauce is great to share over a conversation on the back deck of the Market.

Everyone loves good pizza-by-the-slice. **Pizza Pzzaz** delivers pizza hot from the oven, topped with fresh and unusual ingredients. Their vegetable pizzas are superb, and their Granville Island Special has become a tradition on the Island. To round out your meal, their tasty, low-fat, Gelato Fresco ice cream is sure to hit the spot.

We hope you have enjoyed this tour of the Market we love dearly. We have just scratched the surface of all the wonders available. Uncovering more hidden gems in the Market is a task left for you when you come to visit. Now, let's get cooking!

appetizers

GOAT CHEESE, YAM AND ROASTED GARLIC DIP
WITH HERITAGE TOMATOES

MARKET VEGGIE PLATTER WITH PESTO
AND SUN-DRIED TOMATO DIPS

DUNGENESS CRAB SPRING ROLLS

SESAME, GINGER AND SOY DIP

TUNA TARTARE WITH WASABI MOUSSE

TURKISH SPICED LAMB BALLS

WILD MUSHROOMS IN PUFF PASTRY

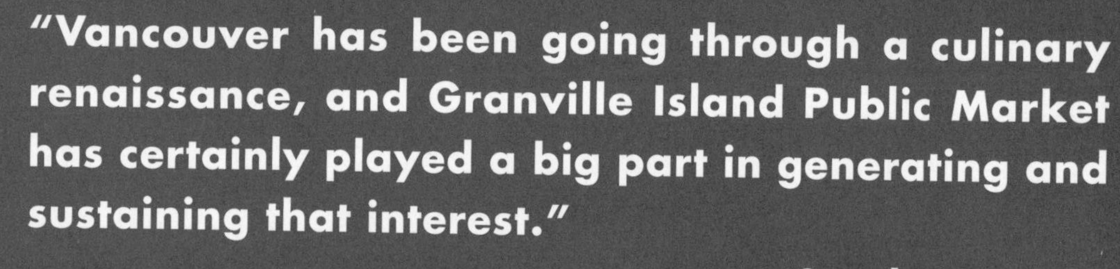
"Vancouver has been going through a culinary renaissance, and Granville Island Public Market has certainly played a big part in generating and sustaining that interest."

—Stephen Wong

MARKET TIME-SAVERS

Apart from supplying top-quality raw ingredients, many Market merchants have been keeping pace with the steadily growing demand for ready-to-eat and ready-to-cook meal solutions for many years. Whether you are hosting a cocktail party or an elaborate family dinner, these value-added Market time-savers will help you spend fewer hours over the stove so you can enjoy more quality time with your friends and loved ones.

Stocks and sauces: Well-crafted stocks, sauces and condiments are obvious flavour-boasting shortcuts to tasty meals. A well-stocked pantry will make short work of many of the recipes in this book. Baste a pork chop with mango chutney from **South China Seas**. Splash your stir-fry with Little Creek dressing from **The Milkman**. Jazz up your halibut with a coconut-lime dressing from the **Stock Market**. The combinations are almost endless.

Pesto: This classic Genoese sauce made from pulverized basil, pine nuts, garlic, Parmesan cheese and olive oil derived its name from the technique with which it was originally made – grinding with a mortar and pesto (pestle). At **Duso's** or **Zara's** you will find many pesto variations, such as sun-dried tomato, cilantro, artichoke and mint. A somewhat unusual favourite of ours is the spicy "skookum pesto" made with locally grown cilantro and jalapeño peppers from one of the day vendors from Vancouver Island, Golda's Fine Foods. Add some pesto to a pot of cooked pasta and, presto, you have an instant, tasty meal. Mix it with sour cream or yogourt and it becomes a quick vegetable dip (see recipe page 46).

Cheese: A cheese plate is an easy way to liven up a party and a delightful end to a great meal. Warm a small round of creamy Brie in the oven and it becomes an instant fondue.

A slice of soft-ripened Camembert on toast topped with a wedge of fresh fig is an elegant and simple hors d'oeuvre. For a little local colour, seek out David Wood's lovingly hand-crafted fresh goat cheese at **Dussa's**. Crust it with coarsely ground pepper or a mélange of freshly chopped herbs, then sit back and enjoy the compliments.

Pâté: Always a hit during the holidays, pâtés are wonderful, stress-free, instant party appetizers, and they come in many flavours. French country-style is usually a blend of chicken or duck liver mixed with pork, garlic and spices. Other varieties available at **Dressed To Go Poultry** include wild boar, duck, pheasant, vegetarian and foie gras and truffle. Pâtés are fabulous when paired with chutneys or preserves such as those from Vancouver Island's Fore and Aft, a regular day vendor. To complete the picture, add a few toasted slices of **Terra's** fruit and nut bread.

Meat and deli products: Marinated skewers of beef, lamb and pork available from any of the Market butchers will take minutes to cook on the barbecue or broiler. Serve them with a salad and a few roasted potatoes. Dinner is ready in less than 30 minutes. Broil or grill a few links of handcrafted sausages and serve them with a one-pot pasta primavera and your kids will love you. Deli meats served on rounds of baguettes or laid out on a tray are surefire hits at any office or potluck party.

Seafood treats: Hot-smoked "Indian candy" (salmon) is a local delicacy that is addictive on its own and magical when sprinkled on a mesclun salad or a cold potato soup. Canapés don't get much better than cream cheese topped with cold-smoked wild sockeye or chinook salmon.

GOAT CHEESE, YAM AND ROASTED GARLIC DIP
with Heritage Tomatoes

Both tangy and slightly sweet, this is a delicious dip for other vegetables, too. Try it on a sandwich instead of mayonnaise.

Preparation time: 75 minutes
Wine pairing: Gamay, light Pinot Noir

Serves 4

1 large yam, pierced all over with a fork
2 tbsp (30 mL) extra-virgin olive oil, divided
salt and pepper to taste
2 large heads of garlic
1 5 oz/150 g pkg David Wood's goat cheese
  or good quality soft goat cheese
1 tbsp (15 mL) lemon juice
1 lb (450 g) multicoloured heritage tomatoes, cut in wedges,
  or cherry, pear or currant tomatoes, whole

Oven: 350°F/180°C

1. Place yam in a small baking pan and drizzle with 1 tbsp/15 mL olive oil. Season well with salt and pepper.
2. Cut top one-third from the garlic heads to expose the cloves. Place the garlic in a small square of aluminum foil and drizzle with remaining olive oil. Season with salt and pepper and wrap securely, but loosely, in the foil.
3. Place garlic in the pan with the yam and bake for 1 hour, or until the yam is soft. Remove the garlic from the foil and allow garlic and yam to cool to room temperature. Peel yam and squeeze roasted garlic pulp from the skins.
4. In a food processor, combine the yam, garlic, goat cheese and lemon juice. Pulse until smooth, then season with salt and pepper.
5. To serve, transfer to a serving bowl and place on a large platter, surrounded by the tomato wedges, or place tomatoes on salad plates and drizzle with the dressing.

KAREN BARNABY

In her witty cookbooks *Pacific Passions* and *Screamingly Good Food*, and in her work in the kitchen at The Fish House in Stanley Park, Karen delights in creating rustic and sensual food that tickles all the senses. A treasure we managed to wrest from Ontario, Karen is a firm believer in giving something back. Hence she is very generous in donating her precious free time to worthwhile causes. One such cause resulted in the *Helping Hands Cookbook*, which she helped edit for Vancouver's Community Kitchens. Of all the foods available at the Public Market, Karen professes to harbour a soft spot for David Wood's goat cheeses (available at Dussa's). After all, Karen and David worked together when Karen was a chef at David's popular food store in Toronto, before they both came to their senses and moved to the West Coast.

MARKET VEGGIE PLATTER

with Pesto and Sun-Dried Tomato Dips

Pesto is a wonderful addition to the modern kitchen pantry. Several Market vendors sell pesto, and occasionally a day table vendor will sell pesto made from locally produced basil, other herbs or vegetables. These red and green dips make a festive pairing and are great for entertaining. In this simple recipe, the use of local, organic produce will elevate the level of the platter and ensure healthy and tasty eating. Be sure to wash all the vegetables carefully before proceeding.

Preparation time: 20 minutes
Wine pairing: Sauvignon Blanc, Pinot Gris

Serves 4

¼ cup (60 mL) basil pesto
2 cups (500 mL) sour cream
2 cups (500 mL) yogourt
juice of 1 lemon
¼ cup (60 mL) sun-dried tomato pesto
1 hothouse cucumber, cut in sticks
4 large carrots, peeled and cut in sticks
1 head of cauliflower, cut in florets
2 heads of broccoli, cut in florets
4 red peppers, seeded and cut in sticks
1 basket cherry tomatoes
½ lb (225 g) small button mushrooms
1 bunch green onions

1. In a serving bowl, combine the basil pesto and half the sour cream, yogourt and lemon juice. Stir well to mix; set aside. In a second serving bowl, combine the sun-dried tomato pesto and the remaining sour cream, yogourt and lemon juice. Stir well to mix; set aside.
2. On a serving platter, place the two bowls of dip in the centre and attractively arrange the vegetables around the edge. If desired, divide the vegetables in half and use a separate platter for each dip. If preparing in advance, soak paper towels in cold water, squeeze gently and drape over the cut vegetables. Cover with plastic film and refrigerate for up to 2 hours.

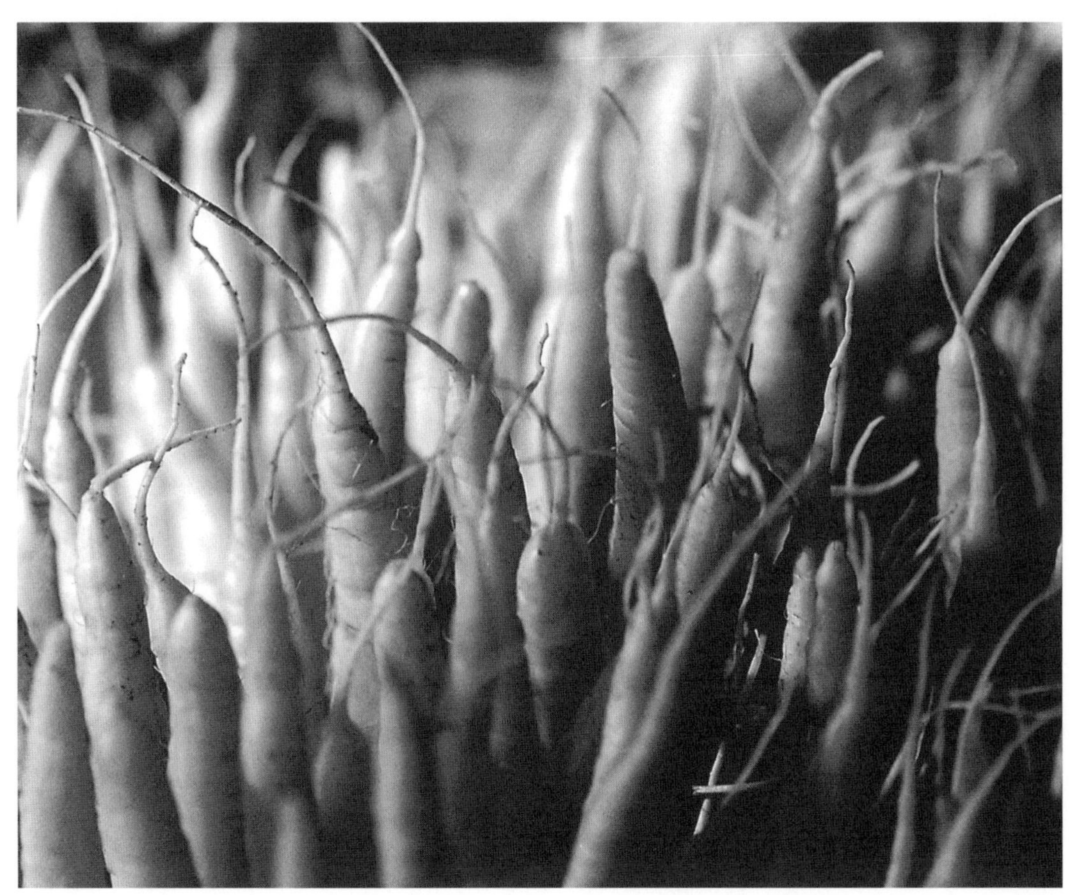

DUNGENESS CRAB SPRING ROLLS

Crabmeat is available from most seafood merchants in the Market. Look for crab with clean white flesh and big chunks of plump leg meat. Alternatively, you can buy a whole crab, boil it in water for 10 minutes, remove the stomach and gills, and clean all the white crabmeat from the body and legs.

Preparation time: 30 minutes
Wine pairing: sparkling wine, Chenin Blanc

Serves 4

½ lb (225 g) Dungeness crabmeat
1 tbsp (15 mL) cilantro, chopped
1 tbsp (15 mL) parsley, chopped
juice and zest of 1 lemon
1 tbsp (15 mL) grainy mustard
¼ cup (60 mL) mayonnaise
1 tsp (5 mL) coriander, ground
1 tbsp (15 mL) ginger, minced
salt and pepper to taste
1 pkg spring roll wrappers
2 tbsp (30 mL) cornstarch, mixed with
  2 tbsp (30 mL) water
canola oil for deep-frying
½ cup (125 mL) Sesame, Ginger and Soy Dip
  (see following recipe)

Deep-frying oil: 360°F/185°C

1. In a medium bowl, pick over the crab for any shell shards and squeeze out excess moisture. Mix in cilantro, parsley, lemon juice and zest, mustard, mayonnaise, coriander, ginger, salt and pepper. Pan-fry a little sample to check seasoning; adjust if necessary.

2. Separate the spring roll wrappers and cover with a lightly dampened towel. Brush the edges with the cornstarch mixture and place a line of filling (about 2 tbsp/30 mL) diagonally across one wrapper. Turn the wrapper so the filling is parallel to you. Pick up one corner and fold over the filling. Shape the filling into a tight log and fold the ends of the spring roll toward the middle. Continue rolling in a tight cylinder. Seal the final flap with a little extra cornstarch mixture. (The wrapper packaging often comes with a helpful diagram for rolling.) Repeat until you have 8 spring rolls. Refrigerate until needed.

3. To a large, heavy-bottomed pot over medium-high heat, add the oil and bring up to temperature. (Place a wooden chopstick in the hot oil; it will bubble vigorously around the chopstick when hot enough.) Add the spring rolls 4 at a time and fry until golden and crisp, about 3 to 4 minutes. Transfer rolls to a plate lined with paper towels to absorb excess oil. Serve warm with Sesame, Ginger and Soy Dip.

SESAME, GINGER AND SOY DIP

This dip makes a great dressing for rice noodles or a wonderful salad dressing and will keep refrigerated for 2 weeks. Add cooked chicken, seafood or vegetables to noodles or salad greens. Toss with the dressing for a tasty main course dish.

Preparation time: 15 minutes

Serves 4

1 tbsp (15 mL) ginger, chopped
1 tsp (5 mL) sesame oil
2 tbsp (30 mL) vegetable oil
1 tbsp (15 mL) honey
¼ tsp (1 mL) chili flakes
¼ cup (60 mL) soy sauce
¼ cup (60 mL) hoisin sauce
1 tbsp (15 mL) sesame seeds, toasted

1. In a food processor, combine the ginger, sesame oil, vegetable oil, honey, chili flakes, soy sauce and hoisin sauce. Pulse until smooth; stir in the sesame seeds. Pour into individual dipping bowls and serve with Dungeness Crab Spring Rolls (see previous recipe).

"It's a great way to enjoy an afternoon and sample foods you wouldn't find in a normal grocery store. The Market showcases healthy eating and makes the great products of our region available to everyone."
—James Walt

TUNA TARTARE
with Wasabi Mousse

Use the freshest sushi-grade tuna you can find. Wednesday to Friday is often the best time to buy fish as merchants stock up for the busy weekend.

Preparation time: 30 minutes
Wine pairing: Pinot Gris, Riesling

Serves 6

Tuna Tartare

- 12 oz (350 g) sushi-grade ahi tuna
- 1 tbsp (15 mL) chives, chopped
- 1 tbsp (15 mL) capers, minced
- 1 tsp (5 mL) ginger, minced
- 3 tbsp (45 mL) canola oil
- 1 tsp (5 mL) sesame oil
- baguette slices, toasted
- chives for garnish

Wasabi Mousse

- 1 cup (250 mL) whipping cream
- 1 tbsp (15 mL) wasabi paste (or to taste)
- 1 tsp (5 mL) lemon juice
- 1 tbsp (15 mL) cilantro, chopped

1. Place tuna in the freezer for 15 minutes to firm up before slicing. Cut the tuna into thin slices, then cut the slices in strips and dice the strips. In a medium-size bowl, combine the chives, capers, ginger, canola oil and sesame oil. Stir in tuna, tossing well to coat.
2. To a medium-size, chilled bowl, add the whipping cream and whisk until soft peaks form. In a small bowl, combine the wasabi paste and lemon juice. Pour mixture into the cream, add the cilantro and rewhip to form soft peaks.
3. To serve, place a small mound of the tuna on a serving plate and spoon the wasabi mousse on the side. Sprinkle the plate with chopped chives and serve with slices of toasted baguette.

JAMES WALT

Raised in a family of great cooks, James knew early on that his career lay in the culinary field. After training at Ontario's prestigious Stratford Chef School, James furthered his craft under the guidance of star chefs Jean-Georges Vongerichten, Jamie Kennedy and Marcella Hagen. He has also travelled extensively in Europe and elsewhere, learning about new techniques, products and the interplay between food and culture. During three and a half years as co-chef at Sooke Harbour House, James developed a passion and deep knowledge for B.C. products. As chef at Araxi in Whistler, he now applies that knowledge to create food for an appreciative world audience all year round. James's razor-sharp wit keeps his co-workers on their toes and helps generate a dynamic environment for the creation of great food that is complemented by one of the best premium wine selections in the province.

TURKISH SPICED LAMB BALLS

These lamb balls, spiced with an aromatic blend of seasonings, make a great appetizer. Serve with a simple dip made with chopped mint, onions, garlic, lemon and yogourt.

Preparation time: 45 minutes
Wine pairing: Cabernet Franc, Chancellor, Sangiovese

Serves 8 to 10

Spice Mix

- 4 tbsp (60 mL) pickling spice mix
- 2 tsp (10 mL) cinnamon
- 2 tsp (10 mL) nutmeg
- 2 tsp (10 mL) fresh mint leaves, chopped
- 2 tsp (10 mL) cumin seeds
- 1 tbsp (15 mL) black pepper-corns

Lamb Balls

- 2¼ lbs (1 kg) ground lamb
- ½ cup (125 mL) parsley, finely chopped
- 4 cloves garlic, minced
- 3 tbsp (45 mL) Turkish herb and spice mix
- ¼ cup (60 mL) fine bread crumbs
- 2 tbsp (30 mL) club soda
- 2 tbsp (30 mL) lemon juice
- 2 tsp (10 mL) salt
- 1 tsp (5 mL) pepper

Oven: 400°F/200°C

1. In a spice grinder (or mortar and pestle), combine the pickling spice mix, cinnamon, nutmeg, mint leaves, cumin and peppercorns. Grind to a fine powder and transfer to a clean jar; seal until needed. Leftover spice mix can be kept for 1 month or longer and is a tasty addition to stews, stir-fries and roasted potatoes.
2. In a large bowl, blend together the lamb, parsley, garlic, spice mix, bread crumbs, soda, lemon juice, salt and pepper. Refrigerate for at least 15 minutes.
3. Rub a little oil on your hands and shape the lamb mixture into small (1 in/2.5 cm) round balls. Place balls on an oiled roasting pan and bake for 20 to 25 minutes or until golden brown. Remove from oven and serve as an appetizer or as a side dish to vegetables and couscous or rice.

DAVID FOOT

David is another native son of Vancouver who has travelled wide and returned home with a renewed enthusiasm for B.C.'s potential as a hot spot on the world culinary map. At the Ambleside Bistro he has implemented his own vision of West Coast cuisine by combining classical procedures with today's contemporary techniques and the best of local products. David's ability to balance new methodology with old-world traditions is a direct result of the European classical training he received at the William Tell and the Prow Restaurant and while working with the Canadian Culinary Olympic Team. David believes that a professional kitchen is like an exquisite meal – all the flavours and ingredients should complement each other and work in harmony.

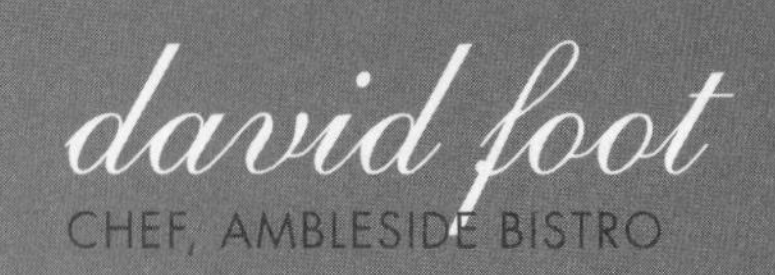

WILD MUSHROOMS IN PUFF PASTRY

If you buy the pastry, this dish is a quick and easy way to impress your guests. Clean the mushrooms well, brushing off any loose soil or twigs. Cut off any area that appears darkened or bruised. Especially check mushrooms like the pine and porcini (cèpe or boletus) for worms and their trails. Wormy mushrooms should be well trimmed.

Preparation time: 60 minutes (with commercial puff pastry)
Wine pairing: Pinot Noir, Pinot Meunier

Serves 4

4 puff pastry shells (4 in/10 cm size)
2 tbsp (30 mL) butter
1 tbsp (15 mL) olive oil
4 shallots, finely chopped
1 tsp (5 mL) fresh thyme, chopped
1 lb (450 g) wild or cultivated mushrooms, coarsely chopped (chanterelle, pine, oyster, porcini, button, shiitake)
salt and pepper to taste
2 tbsp (30 mL) brandy
1 cup (250 mL) whipping cream
¼ cup (60 mL) veal demi-glace or chicken stock

Oven: 400°F/200°C

1. Prepare the puff pastry shells in advance or bake according to package directions.

2. To a large fry pan over medium-high heat, add the butter and oil and heat until the butter starts to sizzle. Add the shallots, thyme and mushrooms. Season well with salt and pepper. Toss to coat and sauté for 2 to 3 minutes or until the mushrooms are hot and sizzling.

3. Remove from heat and add the brandy (carefully, as the brandy may flame up). Return to heat and cook until all the moisture has evaporated and the mushrooms are starting to brown.

4. Add the whipping cream and veal demi-glace to the pan. Lower heat to a simmer and reduce the volume of the sauce by one-third. Season well with salt and pepper.

5. To serve, warm the puff pastry rounds and cut in half. Place bottom on a warm plate and top with one-quarter of the mushroom cream. Top with the puff pastry cap and serve warm.

WILD B.C.
CAULIFLOWER MUSHROOM
$4.50/100g
BEST QUALITY B.C.
SHIITAKE MUSHROOM
$2.65/100g
WILD B.C.
POM-POM Mushrooms
$4.50/100g
WILD B.C.
LOBSTER MUSHROOM
$3.25/100g

"I like the Market because it allows producers to talk directly to customers and exchange information and handling tips. Tourists get to purchase fresh B.C. products in a rustic atmosphere within the city."

—Sean Riley

soups and salads

TOMATO, RED PEPPER, GARLIC AND BREAD SOUP

ROASTED ROMA TOMATO SOUP WITH
PROVENCE CROUTONS

GREEN PEA SOUP WITH CRÈME FRAÎCHE AND SHRIMP

CURRIED CHICKEN WONTON WITH THAI BROTH

MIXED GREENS WITH OVEN-DRIED
TOMATO VINAIGRETTE

PEA SHOOT SALAD ROLLS WITH
CARROT-LIME DRESSING

GRILLED TAMARIND GLAZED QUAIL
OVER MESCLUN GREENS

GRILLED SCALLOP, TOMATO AND AVOCADO SALAD

"When the first-of-the-season fruits and vegetables are ready, the Market always seems to get them first. Sometimes I can't even get them from my regular commercial suppliers. I often go right to the Market vendors to see if they can deliver to my kitchen."

—Todd Konrad

SALAD DAYS

Remember those days when salad meant a jumble of torn iceberg lettuce smothered with commercial Thousand Island dressing? Well, we've come long way since then. Many Market grocers now sell what is commonly called a "mesclun mix," often consisting of a tossed mix of lettuce, radicchio, arugula and leafy Asian greens. For your very own blend, pay a visit to **Fraser Valley Organic Cooperative**, a long-time day vendor. On an average day, depending on the season, they offer a buffet of organic baby lettuce, chickweed, mâche, chicory, mizuma, mustard greens, herbs, edible flowers and more, all sorted into individual baskets. The result is a joyful garden on a plate—one of the prettiest culinary treasures in the Market.

Lettuce: Iceberg is still the flagship lettuce. Much maligned by food snobs for the former indignities it suffered, iceberg still makes the best sandwich lettuce and adds nice texture to a salad mix. Romaine is wonderfully crisp and mild, and is the star of the ever-popular Caesar salad. *Lolla rossa* (Italian for red leaf) is a soft, red-leafed variety, and oak leaf is a mild and fresh tasting green lettuce. Store lettuce loosely wrapped in plastic in the vegetable compartment of your refrigerator. Just before serving, wash and spin dry the leaves, then place in the refrigerator for 10 minutes to crisp them before dressing.

Radicchio: This chicory, often called by its Italian name, radicchio, adds a nice bitter contrast to many salad mixes. Varieties include deep ruby-red, variegated and green-leafed plants. Look for heads that are dense and tightly packed. Avoid heads that have brown, slimy patches on the cut end or along the leaf edges.

Endive: Belgian endive is the most widely known endive, another member of the chicory family. It is a dense-leafed, bitter vegetable, made by blanching (covering with straw or denying sunlight to) young endive plants. Great as a salad, the greens are also wonderful when grilled or braised in a flavourful broth. Curly endive, sometimes called frisée, comes in many forms. Look for bushy heads with a dense white-green batch in the centre.

Asian leafy greens: Local growers in the Pacific Northwest have embraced the cultivation of many Asian greens, and the cool climate is very suitable to their production. Tat soi has dark green, oval leaves that have a pleasing crisp flavour. Mizuma sports deeply cut green leaves with a sweet and satisfying flavour. Mustard greens are pungent, peppery leaves that come in a variety of colours and shapes. All these greens are common in commercial salad mixes.

Kale: This is a hearty member of the Brassicae family, which includes cabbages and broccoli. Red Russian has fine-textured, red-purple leaves with a superb flavour. Peacock kale has beautiful serrated leaves, the colour ranging from soft green to bright purple and pink. Kale contains a wide variety of cancer-fighting phytochemicals and is abundant in antioxidants such as carotene and vitamins A and C.

Herb leaves: Many herb leaves find their way into salad mixes. Mitsuba (Japanese parsley) has a bright and sparkling flavour. Arugula (rocket or roquette) is a spicy green with a distinct nutty, peppery bite. Both nasturtium leaves and flowers have a sharp horseradish taste and are delicious and pretty additions to salads. Dill, fennel and basil are also welcome guests that add complexity to the potpourri.

TOMATO, RED PEPPER, GARLIC AND BREAD SOUP

This is a rustic peasant soup (what else!) from the Mediterranean, thickened and enriched by the addition of good country-style bread. James recommends a crusty French loaf from Terra Breads as the perfect foundation for this delicious soup.

Preparation time: 30 minutes
Wine pairing: Sauvignon Blanc, Pinot Blanc

Serves 4 to 6

2 tbsp (30 mL) extra-virgin olive oil
1 medium onion, chopped
2 tbsp (30 mL) garlic, chopped
6 cups (1.5 L) tomatoes, chopped
2 red or yellow peppers, seeded and chopped
4 cups (1 L) vegetable stock or water
2 cups (500 mL) good French or Italian bread, cubed
2 tbsp (30 mL) basil, chopped
1 tbsp (15 mL) rosemary, chopped
sea salt and pepper to taste
olive oil
Parmesan cheese

1. In a stockpot over medium-high heat, combine the olive oil, onion and garlic and cook until the onion is soft. Add the tomatoes and peppers and sauté for 5 minutes.
2. Pour in the stock and bring to a boil. Add the bread, basil and rosemary. Stir to mix well and cook for 10 to 15 minutes, or until all vegetables are soft and the bread has broken down. Thin the soup with additional stock or water if desired. Season well with salt and pepper. Drizzle a little olive oil into the soup for extra flavour and richness.
3. Transfer to soup bowls and sprinkle freshly grated Parmesan cheese on top. Serve with a slice of fresh bread topped with butter or olive oil.

JAMES BARBER

James's cherubic grin is known to millions of television viewers around the world and his show is now dubbed in 30 or more languages (James in Tagalog?). Watching him on television is like having your own private food guru in your kitchen. On and off the air, he brims with good advice, insightful opinions, wry humour and loads of enthusiasm for eating and cooking. Throughout his illustrious career as a writer and radio and television personality, he has empowered and mentored many young culinary stars in Vancouver. James loves quality ingredients and can often be seen strolling around the Market laden with bags stuffed with bread, cheese, greens and heritage tomatoes – a veritable shopping list of good taste. His love of food is infectious and his philosophy is simple: "Just roll up your sleeves and get in there."

ROASTED ROMA TOMATO SOUP

with Provence Croutons

Alessandra claims this soup originated from an accidental deep-roasting of tomatoes that was salvaged into their daily soup special. Out of chaos a sublime soup was born. The taste is the essence of tomato and a reminder of the south of France, all in the same bowl. Herbes de Provence is often available as a dried herb mixture.

Preparation time: 90 minutes
Wine pairing: Sauvignon Blanc, Semillon

Serves 4 to 6

Croutons

1 cup (250 mL) French baguette cubes (½ inch/1 cm)
½ cup (125 mL) butter, melted
1 tsp (5 mL) dried chili peppers, crushed
1 tbsp (15 mL) garlic, minced
2 tbsp (30 mL) parsley, minced
3 tbsp (45 mL) dried herbes de Provence, divided (thyme, rosemary, bay leaf, basil and savory)

Soup

3 lbs (1.3 kg) Roma tomatoes, halved
½ cup (125 mL) extra-virgin olive oil
salt and pepper to taste
4 cups (1 L) water
1 whole garlic bulb, peeled
2 tbsp (30 mL) fresh basil, chopped
1 tomato, chopped
extra-virgin olive oil for drizzling

Oven: 300°F/150°C

1. In a small bowl, combine bread, butter, chilies, garlic, parsley and 1 tbsp/15 mL herbes de Provence. Transfer to a baking sheet and bake for 15 minutes or until lightly golden. Remove from oven and reserve.
2. On a baking sheet, place tomatoes skin side down; drizzle with olive oil and sprinkle with remaining herbes de Provence, salt and pepper. Bake for 1 hour or until tomatoes are soft and wrinkled.
3. Using a spatula, scrape roasted tomatoes and all the pan juices, oil and seasonings from the baking sheet into a medium saucepan. Add water and peeled garlic cloves; stir well. Bring mixture to a boil over high heat. Reduce heat to low and simmer for 20 minutes. Remove from heat and purée mixture in a blender or food processor until smooth. Strain soup through a fine sieve, pressing well to remove all of the juice from the tomato skin and seeds. Season with salt and pepper.
4. Ladle hot soup into bowls and top each with a spoonful of basil, chopped tomatoes and the croutons. Finish with a drizzle of olive oil and serve immediately.

ALESSANDRA & JEAN-FRANCIS QUAGLIA

Alessandra and Jean-Francis met while working in Nice, France, in 1990. Alessandra was doing a stint at the Hotel Negresco, where Jean-Francis happened to work. The chemistry was there, and after the season, the two went to work at Le Patalain, owned by his mother, Suzanne Quaglia, a renowned Marseilles chef. The pair decided to return to Alessandra's hometown of Toronto to get married and then to relocate to Vancouver. Time was spent in many fine restaurants, including Le Coq d'Or and the Raintree, before they found just the right spot, on 10th Avenue in Kitsilano, to venture out on their own. Returning to family roots while realizing a shared dream, they opened Provence Mediterranean Bistro in December of 1997. Now, practically every summer, Momma Suzanne comes to visit and the happy, reunited family prepares a special menu for the restaurant to celebrate the occasion.

EXECUTIVE CHEF, BEACHSIDE CAFÉ

GREEN PEA SOUP

with Crème Fraîche and Shrimp

This is a very simple, elegant treatment for peas. Make the soup from fresh peas in season or use frozen peas for a respectable alternative. To clean the leeks, split and rinse them under cold water to remove any trace of grit.

Preparation time: 20 minutes
Wine pairing: Fruity Sauvignon Blanc, un-oaked Chardonnay

Serves 10 to 12

2 tbsp (30 mL) butter
2 medium onions, diced
2 tbsp (30 mL) garlic, minced
2 leeks (white part only), thinly sliced
2¼ lbs (1 kg) frozen peas (one large bag)
3 qts (3 L) chicken or vegetable stock
sea salt and pepper to taste
1 cup (250 mL) crème fraîche or sour cream
2 cups (500 mL) shrimp, peeled, deveined and cooked

1. In a large saucepan over medium-high heat, melt the butter until sizzling. Add the onions, garlic and leeks and sauté for 2 to 3 minutes or until the onions are transparent. Add the peas and stock and bring to a boil. Reduce heat and simmer for 5 minutes or until the peas are tender.
2. Strain the soup and cool to room temperature, or use an ice bath to quickly cool the soup if it is to be served cold. Blend the solids in a food mill or processor, adding a little liquid to make a smooth purée. Reserve the extra broth for use at another time.
3. Season with salt and pepper to taste. Serve soup hot or cold. Garnish with a dollop of crème fraîche and a sprinkling of shrimp.

CURRIED CHICKEN WONTON

with Thai Broth

This light and intensely spiced broth is both healthy and satisfying. For a richer version, Nathan adds a can of coconut milk to the broth. The wonton skins usually come in packages of 50 and are available in the Market from South China Seas. Freeze any unused wrappers for later use.

Preparation time: 40 minutes
Wine pairing: Gewürztraminer, Riesling

Serves 4 to 6

Wonton

1 large chicken breast, diced
4 large water chestnuts, chopped
1 green onion, finely chopped
¼ cup (60 mL) pine nuts, toasted
2 tbsp (30 mL) dried currants
1 tbsp (15 mL) curry powder
salt and pepper to taste
1 pkg wonton wrappers
1 large egg, beaten

Broth

4 cups (1 L) chicken stock
1 stalk lemongrass, coarsely chopped
4 medium shallots, halved
10 slices fresh galangal root
2 fresh cilantro stems, chopped
5 kaffir lime leaves, chopped
2 tbsp (30 mL) fish sauce
2 tbsp (30 mL) lime juice
1 tbsp (15 mL) palm sugar
4 small green chilies
fresh cilantro sprigs for garnish

1. In a small bowl, combine chicken, water chestnuts, green onion, pine nuts, currants and curry powder. Season with salt and pepper.
2. Take one wonton wrapper and place a small teaspoonful of the chicken mixture in the middle. Brush edges with the beaten egg, fold to form a triangle and pinch to seal. Take two corners of the triangle and press together with a small amount of egg wash to form a crescent. Set aside on a baking sheet lined with wax paper and continue with the remaining wontons. Refrigerate until ready to use.
3. In a medium pot, bring the stock to a boil. In a food processor, chop the lemongrass and shallots together until finely minced. Add the lemongrass mixture, galangal, cilantro stems and kaffir lime to the stock. Reduce heat and simmer for 10 minutes. Season with the fish sauce, lime juice, palm sugar and chilies.
4. Add the wontons to the soup and simmer, uncovered, until the filling is firm and cooked through, about 5 minutes. Ladle the broth and wontons into serving bowls and garnish with cilantro leaves.

todd konrad

CHEF AND OWNER, ZINFANDEL RESTAURANT

MIXED GREENS
with Oven-Dried Tomato Vinaigrette

Todd loves to serve this salad with a side dish of grilled salmon for an elegant lunch.

Preparation time: Vinaigrette, 60 minutes; Salad, 15 minutes
Wine pairing: Pinot Blanc, Pinot Gris, Semillon

Serves 4

Vinaigrette

1 beef steak tomato, sliced
juice of 1 lemon
½ cup (125 mL) extra-virgin olive oil
salt and pepper to taste

Salad

2 cups (500 mL) arugula, torn into bite-size pieces
2 cups (500 mL) mesclun salad mix
2 cups (500 mL) mixed berries (strawberry, blueberry, raspberry)
croutons (optional, see sidebar)

CROUTONS

A nice addition to salads or soups, croutons are also a great way to use up leftover bread. Cut the bread (or bagels, or polenta) into small cubes. Drizzle with a little extra-virgin olive oil, a spoonful of minced garlic and your favourite chopped herbs. Season well with salt and pepper and place on a baking sheet. Bake in a 350°F/180°C oven for 7 to 8 minutes or until golden brown. Remove from oven and allow to cool.

Oven: 300°F/150°C

1. Place the tomato slices on a baking sheet lined with parchment paper. Bake for 1 hour or until the slices are dry. Remove from oven and chop finely, reserving 4 slices for garnish.
2. In a small bowl, combine the tomatoes and lemon juice. Whisk in olive oil in a steady stream until well mixed. Season with salt and pepper and set aside.
3. In a salad bowl, toss the arugula, mesclun and half the vinaigrette mixture. Transfer salad to serving plates, top with the berries and drizzle remaining dressing around the salad. Garnish each salad with a slice of dried tomato.

TODD KONRAD

A stint at the Hong Kong Shangri-La's Aberdeen Marina Club combined with tours of duty at a "who's who" of B.C.'s regional bastions of good taste – Chateau Whistler, Sooke Harbour House, the Hotel Vancouver and the Wickaninnish Inn – have prepared Todd Konrad well for the realization of his lifelong ambition: to be at the helm of his own restaurant. In the fall of 1999 his dream came true and Zinfandel opened its doors. These days you will find him dividing his time between Zinfandel's compact kitchen and its cozy dining room, juggling between executing the signature dishes that he has created and talking to diners about the source of his inspiration.

PEA SHOOT SALAD ROLLS

with Carrot-Lime Dressing

Other greens such as shredded napa cabbage, savoy cabbage, kale and watercress can be substituted for the pea shoots in this versatile recipe. Pea shoots are the tender tops of snow pea plants. They have a nutty pealike flavour and are excellent in salads or simply sautéed with butter and served as you would spinach.

Preparation time: 10 minutes
Wine pairing: Pinot Blanc, Riesling, Semillon

Serves 6

Dressing

1 tbsp (15 mL) rice vinegar
¼ cup (60 mL) lime juice
1 cup (250 mL) carrot juice
1 serrano chili, seeded and chopped
2 tsp (10 mL) minced ginger
salt and pepper to taste

Salad Rolls

6 8 in/20 cm round dried rice paper sheets
3 cups (750 mL) pea shoots or mesclun salad mix, tightly packed
1 cup (250 mL) bean sprouts, tightly packed
¼ cup (60 mL) sliced almonds, toasted

1. In a food processor or blender, combine all dressing ingredients and blend until smooth. Season with salt and pepper to taste.
2. Into a large bowl filled with boiling water, dip a sheet of rice paper until it softens, about 5 to 10 seconds. Remove; place on clean surface and pat dry with a towel. Place a portion of the pea shoots or salad mix and the bean sprouts on lower half of rice wrapper and sprinkle with almonds. Bring side edges of wrapper over filling and roll into a tight cylinder, pressing gently to seal. Repeat with remaining rice paper sheets.
3. To serve, cut rolls diagonally in half, divide and arrange on serving plates. Drizzle with dressing. Alternatively, pour dressing into small ramekins and use as a dipping sauce.

ASIAN VEGETABLES

Many nutritious and easy-to-cook Chinese greens belonging to the Brassicae family are available at many Market vendors. **Bok choy**, with its fleshy, thick white stalks and dark green, shiny, rumpled leaves, is the most common. It is are best cooked gently, braised in stock. **Shanghai bok choy**, its close cousin, sporting pale green, spoon-shaped leaves and thinner stalks, is great in stir-fries or braised whole as a side vegetable. **Gai lan**, or Chinese broccoli, reputedly a good source of calcium, iron and vitamins A and C, has white flowers with dull, waxy, jade green stems and leaves and a rich, nutty flavor. **Siu choy** and **Tientsin cabbage** (also called napa cabbage) are the staple greens of northern China.

GRILLED TAMARIND GLAZED QUAIL

over Mesclun Greens

Marinating with honey gives the quail a charred and crisp exterior, which contrasts wonderfully with the sweet quail meat. Try using brown sugar or maple syrup in place of the honey.

Preparation time: Marinade, 3 hours or overnight; Quail, 20 minutes
Wine pairing: Cabernet Franc, Merlot

Serves 4 to 6

½ cup (125 mL) shallots, minced
½ cup (125 mL) soy sauce
1 tbsp (15 mL) tamarind paste
2 tbsp (30 mL) honey
1 tbsp (15 mL) garlic, minced
2 tbsp (30 mL) five-spice powder
¼ cup (60 mL) cider vinegar
1 tbsp (15 mL) ginger, minced
1 cup (250 mL) water
8 whole quails, cut in half
4 cups (1 L) mesclun greens
2 tbsp (30 mL) extra-virgin olive oil
salt and pepper to taste

Grill: medium-hot

1. In a small, nonreactive saucepan, prepare marinade by combining shallots, soy sauce, tamarind paste, honey, garlic, five-spice powder, vinegar, ginger and water. Bring to a boil and cook for 2 minutes, stirring occasionally. Remove from heat, cool and strain; reserve liquid.
2. In a large bowl, combine quails and marinade until quails are well coated. Refrigerate and marinate for at least 3 hours but no more than 12 hours, turning occasionally.
3. On an oiled grill, cook the drained quail until golden brown on the outside but still juicy inside, about 2 to 3 minutes per side. Baste with additional marinade while cooking.
4. In a mixing bowl, combine the mesclun greens and olive oil; season with salt and pepper and toss to mix. To serve, divide salad among plates and top each with the grilled quail. Serve 2 pieces of halved quail on salad as an appetizer or 4 with oven-roasted potatoes and vegetables as a main course.

TAMARIND

Tamarind is a favoured sour element in Southeast Asian cooking. Its processed pulp, partially dried and wrapped in plastic, is sold at South China Seas. The fresh, brown, hard-shelled, beanlike fruits are sometimes available at Market produce vendors as well. To prepare, soak the pulp in hot water in a nonreactive bowl for about 15 minutes, use your fingers to separate the pulp from the fibres and strain mixture through a fine sieve – and it's ready to use.

GRILLED SCALLOP, TOMATO AND AVOCADO SALAD

This dish pairs the silky texture of sea scallops with the bite of ripe tomatoes and avocados in a lively lime dressing.

Preparation time: 30 minutes
Wine pairing: Un-oaked Chardonnay, Sauvignon Blanc

Serves 4

Vinaigrette

- 2 tbsp (30 mL) lime juice
- ¼ cup (60 mL) extra-virgin olive oil
- 2 tbsp (30 mL) Italian parsley, minced
- 1 tsp (5 mL) lemon balm, minced, or lemon zest
- 1 tsp (5 mL) Dijon mustard
- salt and pepper to taste

Salad

- 4 yellow tomatoes
- 4 red tomatoes
- 2 avocados
- 1 tbsp (15 mL) fresh lemon juice
- 1 tbsp (15 mL) sour cream
- 1 tbsp (15 mL) chives, chopped
- 1 tsp (5 mL) Tabasco sauce
- 8 sea scallops
- 1 tbsp (15 mL) sunflower oil
- 2 cups (500 mL) mesclun greens
- fresh herbs for garnish

Grill: hot

1. In a small bowl, combine the lime juice, olive oil, parsley, lemon balm, mustard, salt and pepper. Set aside.
2. Slice the yellow tomatoes thinly. Season with salt and pepper and set aside.
3. Remove the stems from the red tomatoes. Cut a crosswise X on the skin of each tomato and place in boiling water for 10 seconds. Transfer to a bowl of ice water and cool. Drain, peel and cut the tomatoes in half. Squeeze out seeds and juice, cut into ¼ in/5 mm cubes and set aside.
4. Cut the avocados in half. Remove the stone and skin from each and cut into ¼ in/5 mm cubes. Place in a medium bowl. Sprinkle with lemon juice and add sour cream, chives, Tabasco, diced red tomato, salt and pepper.
5. Cut scallops in half. Brush with sunflower oil and season with salt and pepper. Cook over a hot grill for approximately 2 minutes per side. Remove and set aside.
6. Arrange the yellow tomato slices in a circular pattern in the centre of the plate. Place a few mesclun greens in the centre of each circle and spoon tomato-avocado mixture on top. Place 4 scallops on each salad and drizzle with the vinaigrette. Garnish with fresh-herb sprigs.

shellfish

OYSTERS ON THE HALF SHELL WITH ARTICHOKE AND CHAMPAGNE DRESSING

GRILLED OYSTERS WITH SMOKED PAPRIKA MAYONNAISE

STEAMED OYSTERS WITH BLACK BEAN AND GARLIC-BRANDY SAUCES

CURRIED COCONUT SHELLFISH STEW

GOLDEN MUSSEL HOT POT

ORANGE AND FIVE-SPICE MANILA CLAMS

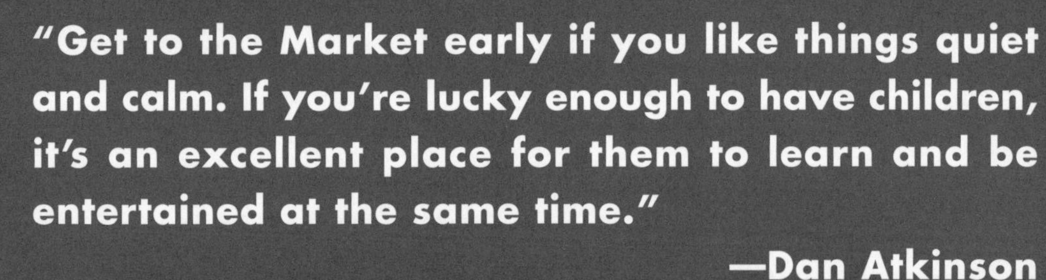

"Get to the Market early if you like things quiet and calm. If you're lucky enough to have children, it's an excellent place for them to learn and be entertained at the same time."

—Dan Atkinson

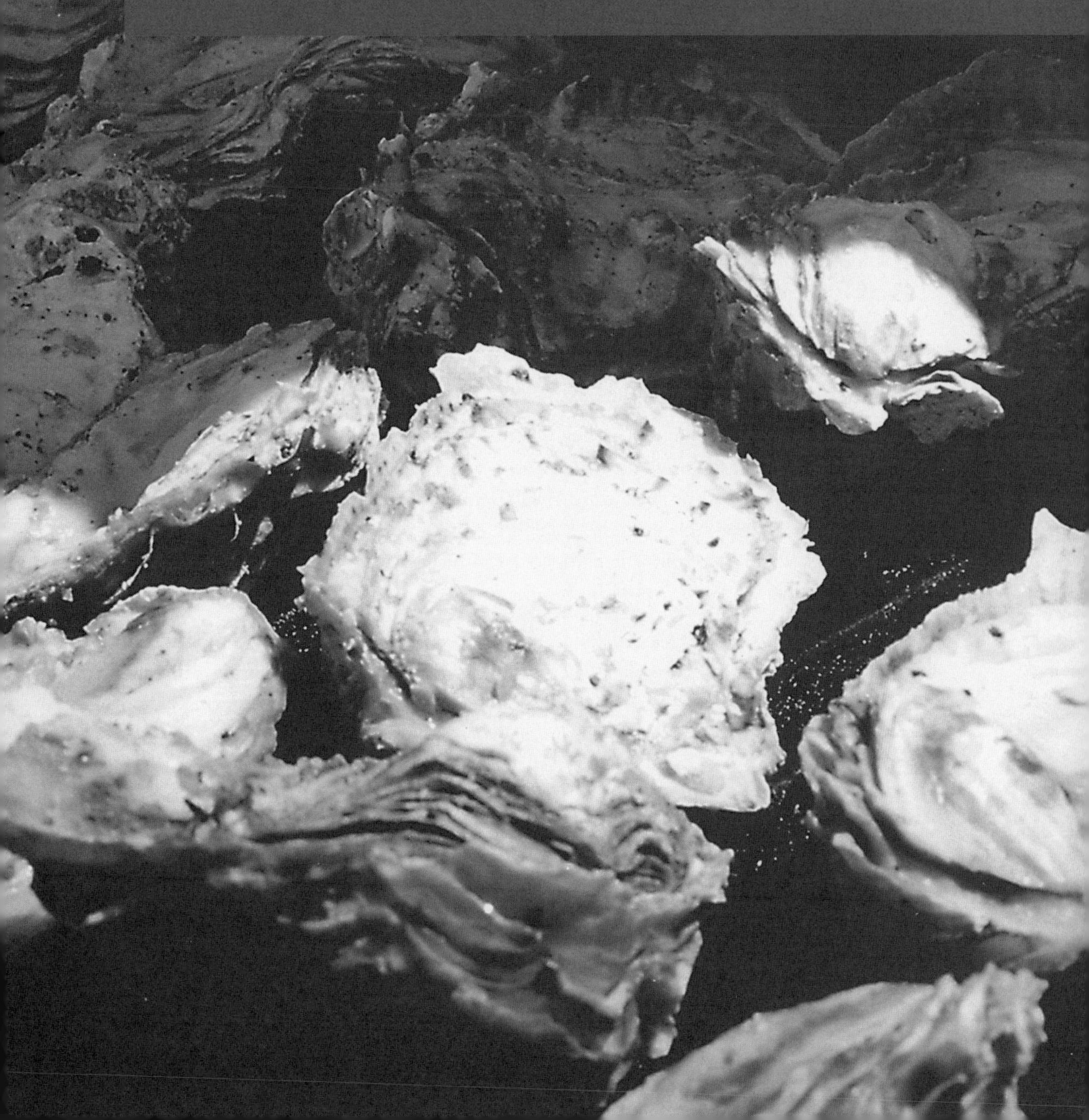

SHELLFISH CARE AND HANDLING

A great part of shopping at the Market is the readily available expertise of the merchants and their staff. They can always be counted on if you want to know more about the origin and pedigree of the many different varieties of crustaceans and mollusks from our local waters. All shellfish should be handled carefully and should, ideally, be bought the same day they are consumed. If you have to store shellfish for a while, avoid holding them in fresh water, as this will shock and kill them. Instead, rinse the shellfish in cold water and transfer them to a storage container lined with a raised rack and topped with ice. This will keep them fresh and plump until you cook them. Large specimens will take a little longer to cook than smaller ones. Remove them from the heat as soon as the shells open for best results, as they will shrink and toughen if overcooked. On hot days, ask the merchant for ice to pack around your shellfish to ensure they make the journey home in prime condition.

Oysters: Oyster cultivation is a booming business on the West Coast. We farm varieties from Europe and Asia along with native species, all with great success. When shopping for oysters, try to buy them in the shell whenever possible. Pick those that are hefty and firmly closed. Cover them with a wet towel in the coldest part of your refrigerator and they will keep nicely for two or three days. You can now buy freshly shucked oysters in convenient plastic tubs. These are great for cooking, but if you intend to eat them raw, small live ones in the shell are the only choice. Check the container for a sell-by date and choose the freshest possible.

Clams: These tasty bivalves are commonly farmed or harvested along the coast of the Pacific Northwest. They are a little hardier than mussels but are handled in much the same manner. Two main varieties are cultivated, the Pacific Littleneck and the Manila Clam. A third clam, the geoduck, is gaining in importance both as a locally consumed product and as an export.

Mussels: The Atlantic blue mussel is commonly cultivated in our water, often imported from Prince Edward Island. Native West Coast golden mussels are a recent addition to the Market. Try to buy mussels on the day you want to cook them.

Scallops: Disklike, cream-coloured to beige-pink, scallop meat is actually the abductor muscle that holds the two parts of the shell together. Bay scallops, generally smaller in size, and sea scallops, their larger cousins, are best if they are sweet-smelling, moist and plump and possess a translucent, onyxlike sheen. Many of the best scallops are frozen at sea, so don't hesitate to buy them if they are glazed with ice and frost-burn free. Large scallops are best seared over high heat on both sides until crusted golden yet medium–cooked inside. Our pretty local pink swimming scallops should be bought live and can be eaten whole as you would clams and mussels.

Prawns: Local prawns and shrimps are some of the finest available anywhere, their flesh sweet, delicate and tender. Spot prawns are the largest local variety (the biggest are 10 to a pound). Two smaller varieties, coon-striped and side-striped shrimp, are also available. Spot prawns must be served very fresh to remain crisp and succulent; sautéing and dry cooking are the best methods of preparation.

Squid: Squid is often billed as calamari on restaurant menus. To ensure that it's tender, squid must be cooked either very quickly (1 to 2 minutes) or braised slowly for a long time (more than 20 minutes). Anything in between tends to render it tough and almost unpalatable. Fresh squid will have a clean white flesh and smell of the sea. A pink tinge may be a sign that the product is less than optimal and the skin pigments are starting to break down.

OYSTERS ON THE HALF SHELL
with Artichoke and Champagne Dressing

Fresh Pacific and Atlantic oysters are an important product farmed off the coast of British Columbia. The Northwest Coast is flush with rich and clean Arctic waters, creating a perfect environment for raising shellfish.

Preparation time: 20 minutes
Wine pairing: Blanc de Blanc or Riesling sparkling wine

Serves 2 to 4

12 fresh B.C. oysters, shucked, juice saved
2 artichoke hearts (canned or fresh, blanched), minced
2 tbsp (30 mL) shallots, minced
juice of 1 lemon
pepper to taste
½ cup (125 mL) champagne or sparkling wine

HOW TO OPEN AN OYSTER

Hold the oyster firmly, flat side up, with one hand covered with a thick towel. This will prevent possible injury if you slip. With your other hand, insert a sturdy oyster knife carefully but forcefully into the hinge of the oyster. Push and twist until you can feel the top shell coming loose. Slide the tip of the oyster knife along one side of the oyster between the shells until you come in contact with the abductor muscle that holds the shells together. Cut the abductor muscle under the top shell and remove the top shell. Then, cut the abductor muscle beneath the oyster to free it from the bottom shell. Retain the juice to pour over the freshly shucked oyster, or add to any sauce or broth.

1. Shuck the oysters and strain the juices into a small bowl. Reserve the oysters and shells.
2. In a small mixing bowl, combine the oyster juice, artichokes, shallots, lemon juice, pepper and champagne.
3. To serve, place the oysters on a platter or tray lined with crushed ice or coarse salt. Spoon a little of the dressing on each oyster and eat immediately.

DAN ATKINSON

Dan was born in Edmonton, grew up in Winnipeg and found his calling while working part–time in a kitchen in Yellowknife more than 20 years ago. Realizing his passion for cooking, he attended formal training at BCIT and went on to work for some of the Lower Mainland's best restaurants, including Café de Medici and La Toque Blanche, before taking the helm at Salmon House on the Hill. Down-to-earth, self-effacing and possessing a dry sense of humour, he claims his philosophy of cooking is rooted in his desire to experiment with flavours. "Everyone puts a personal stamp on their cooking," says Dan. "The same food can be cooked by two chefs and taste completely different, yet both can be excellent." But we all know that it takes much more than a little epicurious alchemy to turn a prairie boy into the chef of one of the most notable seafood houses on the West Coast. A clue? The early bird gets the fish.

GRILLED OYSTERS
with Smoked Paprika Mayonnaise

Use 1 qt/1 L of freshly shucked oysters for this dish. Available at most of the seafood shops, shucked oysters are excellent in pan-fries, chowders, gratins and pies. In the Market, smoked paprika is available at South China Seas. Carol likes to use Fanny Bay Oysters from Vancouver Island.

Preparation time: 30 minutes
Wine pairing: Pinot Gris, Riesling sparkling wine

Serves 4

Mayonnaise

1 egg yolk
1 tbsp (15 mL) Dijon mustard
2 tbsp (30 mL) white wine vinegar
juice and zest of 1 lemon
1 small shallot, minced
1 cup (250 mL) vegetable oil
1 tbsp (15 mL) smoked paprika or chili powder
salt and pepper to taste
Tabasco sauce to taste
Worcestershire sauce to taste

Oysters

2 qts (2 L) water
1 onion, peeled and diced
1 leek, white part only, thinly sliced
juice of 1 lemon
1 qt (1 L) shucked oysters (about 12 large)
1 tbsp (15 mL) olive oil
8 wooden skewers, soaked in cold water
fresh lemon juice for drizzling
fresh cilantro sprigs for garnish

Grill: hot

1. In a food processor, process the egg yolk, mustard, vinegar, lemon juice and zest and shallot. With the machine still running, add the oil in a steady stream until a thick paste is formed. Remove mixture from processor and season with smoked paprika, salt and pepper. Add a dash each of Tabasco and Worcestershire sauce and stir to mix. Cover and refrigerate until ready to use.
2. In a large saucepan, combine the water, onion, leek and juice of second lemon. Bring to a boil, reduce heat and simmer for 10 minutes. Add the shucked oysters and return to a boil. With a slotted spoon, remove oysters from the broth and drain on a plate lined with paper towels. (Strain and reserve broth as a stock for soups or chowders.)
3. Place the oysters in a small bowl and drizzle with the oil. Season with salt and pepper and toss gently to coat.
4. Lay three oysters on a flat surface and run a skewer through the top third of the thickest part of each oyster. Run a second skewer through the delicate bottom of the oyster to make 1 serving. Repeat with remaining oysters to make 4 double skewers.
5. On a hot grill, cook the oysters until lightly charred, about 1 minute per side. Transfer to a warm plate, drizzle with fresh lemon juice and spoon the smoked paprika mayonnaise on and around the oysters. Garnish with fresh cilantro sprigs.

CAROL CHOW

Carol Chow has been the executive chef at the Beachside Café since 1991. A top student from the Dubrulle International Culinary Institute, she was recruited to Umberto's Settebello Ristorante upon graduation and went on to become chef at the renowned Bishop's Restaurant for three and a half years. An avid supporter of regional cuisine, Carol played an active role in the creation of Xclusively BC, a foundation of local chefs that raises funds to provide culinary scholarships for aspiring young cooks. A frequent Market shopper, she believes in using the finest fresh local products to create meals that are simple and intensely flavoured.

STEAMED OYSTERS

with Black Bean and Garlic-Brandy Sauces

This is a great way to enjoy local cultivated beach oysters. Select large ones (sometimes they are as big as your hand), as they are meatier.

Preparation time: 30 minutes
Wine pairing: Riesling, Chenin Blanc

Serves 4

12 large oysters, shucked and left on the half shell, (reserve liquid from the shells)

Black Bean Sauce

3 tbsp (45 mL) black bean sauce
1 tbsp (15 mL) hot bean sauce
1 tbsp (15 mL) light soy sauce
1 tbsp (15 mL) peanut oil
2 tsp (10 mL) garlic, minced
1 tbsp (15 mL) cilantro, finely chopped

Garlic-Brandy Sauce

1 tbsp (15mL) vegetable oil
¼ cup (60 mL) garlic, finely chopped
2 tbsp (30 mL) brandy
1 tbsp (15 mL) green onions, finely sliced

1. In a large wok over high heat, bring 3 cups/750 mL water to a boil. Place steamer rack or basket in wok and cover. Arrange all the oysters, on their half shells, on a heat-resistant platter.
2. In a small bowl, combine all ingredients for Black Bean Sauce except cilantro. Mix well. Spoon onto 6 of the oysters and sprinkle with cilantro.
3. To make Garlic-Brandy Sauce, to a small fry pan over high heat add oil and heat until very hot. Add garlic and stir–fry until fragrant. Add brandy carefully, as the pan may flame. If it does not flame, ignite brandy and allow alcohol to burn off.
4. Spoon brandy sauce evenly over the 6 remaining oysters. Garnish with a sprinkle of green onions.
5. Place platter of oysters in preheated steamer and cover. Steam for 4 to 5 minutes or until oysters are warmed through and firm to the touch. Serve immediately.

CURRIED COCONUT SHELLFISH STEW

This versatile dish can be just as tasty made with other seafood such as salmon, halibut, oysters or any combination of your choice. Adding vegetables such as blanched potatoes, celery, corn or carrots can turn this into a quick and easy one-pot dinner. Use the larger cultivated Japanese scallops for the best results. Pink swimming scallops also work well but should be added near the end, as they cook very quickly.

Preparation time: 20 minutes
Wine pairing: Riesling, Gewürztraminer, Chenin Blanc

Serves 4

1 14 oz/398 mL can unsweetened coconut milk
6 thin slices of ginger root
1 tbsp (15 mL) lemongrass, thinly sliced
2 tsp (10 mL) Madras curry powder (or to taste)
1 lb (450 g) fresh clams, scrubbed and rinsed
1 lb (450 g) fresh mussels, debearded, scrubbed and rinsed
12 fresh cultivated scallops (in the shell)
¼ cup (60 mL) red bell pepper, diced
3 tbsp (45 mL) fresh basil, cut into thin strips
1 tbsp (15 mL) fresh lime juice (or to taste)
1 tbsp (15 mL) fish sauce (or to taste)
1 tsp (5 mL) sugar
salt and freshly ground pepper

1. In a large, heavy saucepan or wok over medium-high heat, heat coconut milk until just boiling. Add ginger, lemongrass and curry powder; cook for 1 minute, stirring to mix thoroughly. Add clams, mussels and scallops; cover and cook until they are open, about 5 to 7 minutes. Shaking the saucepan occasionally will help the process.
2. With a slotted spoon, remove open shellfish and continue to cook for 1 to 2 minutes or until all the shellfish are open. Discard any shellfish that remain closed by this time.
3. Return liquid to a gentle boil and add the red pepper, basil, lime juice, fish sauce and sugar. Season with salt and pepper and simmer for 1 minute. Return shellfish to warm through. Serve immediately.

GOLDEN MUSSEL HOT POT

Japanese-style preparation turns succulent mussels into a dish full of subtle and intriguing flavours that highlight the natural perfection of the shellfish.

Preparation time: Dashi, 12 hours or overnight; Hot Pot, 20 minutes
Wine pairing: Pinot Gris, dry Riesling

Serves 4 to 6

Dashi

- 6 qts (6 L) cold water
- 1 4 in/10 cm strip kombu seaweed (kelp)
- ¼ cup (60 mL) shaved bonito (dried tuna flakes)
- ½ cup (125 mL) mirin (sweet rice wine)
- ½ cup (125 mL) light soy sauce

Hot Pot

- 3 qts (3 L) Dashi
- 3 medium shallots, peeled and sliced
- 2 tbsp (30 mL) ginger, grated
- 1 cup (250 mL) sake
- 5 lbs (2.25 kg) B.C. golden mussels, scrubbed and debearded
- 1 red pepper, seeded and thinly sliced
- 1 yellow pepper, seeded and thinly sliced
- 1 bunch green onions, sliced on diagonal
- ½ cup (125 mL) pickled daikon radish, diced, or shredded cabbage
- 1 pkg (1 lb/450 g) precooked soba noodles

1. In a large bowl, combine 3 qts/3 L cold water and seaweed and soak overnight. The next day, drain and discard water.
2. In a stockpot over medium-high heat, combine 3 qts/3 L fresh cold water, seaweed and bonito flakes. Bring to a boil and remove from the heat. Let stand for 10 minutes and strain into a clean pot; place over high heat and bring to a simmer. Reduce heat, add mirin and soy sauce and simmer for 2 minutes. Remove from heat, cool and reserve.
3. In a large hot pot (or wok or a large stockpot with a lid), combine Dashi, shallots, ginger, sake and mussels. Place over medium-high heat for 5 to 7 minutes or until the mussels have all opened. Discard any mussels that do not open. Spread red pepper, yellow pepper, green onions, daikon radish and noodles over top of the mussels. Cover and bring pot to the table for serving. Provide an extra bowl for discarding empty shells.

ROBERT CLARK

Stand at the north shore of the Market and gaze across False Creek (or, better yet, take one of the quaint little ferries across) and you will see one of Vancouver's finest (and shortest-named) seafood restaurants, C. This is where you will find Montreal-born Robert Clark in his domain. Heralded by the local and international press as a rising star of the Vancouver culinary scene, Robert is quick to attribute his success to the many Canadian culinary notables, such as Jamie Kennedy, Michael Bonaccini, Mark Thuet and Adam Busby, who have inspired him during his career. A regular shopper at the Market, Robert's favourite time of the year is the fall, when the crowds have died down from the summer bustle and harvest produce and delicacies are still arriving in the stores.

EXECUTIVE CHEF, C RESTAURANT

ORANGE AND FIVE-SPICE MANILA CLAMS

The sweet and sour flavour of orange and lemon juice is gently enhanced with licorice-scented five-spice powder, a mixture of fennel, cloves, star anise, Szechuan peppercorns and cinnamon. This dish may be served warm or at room temperature.

Preparation time: 10 minutes
Wine pairing: Ehrenfelser, Kerner, dry Riesling

Serves 4 to 6

3 tbsp (45 mL) olive oil
1 tbsp (15 mL) five-spice powder
zest of 2 oranges
4 lbs (1.8 kg) Manila clams
1 cup (250 mL) orange juice
juice of 1 lemon
1 tbsp (15 mL) butter, chilled (optional)
cilantro or parsley, chopped, for garnish
freshly ground pepper to taste

1. To a wok or deep-sided sauté pan over medium-high heat, add the oil and five-spice powder and cook briefly until fragrant. Add the orange zest and cook for an additional 30 seconds. Toss in the clams and stir-fry to heat through. Add the orange and lemon juices. Cover and cook for 4 to 5 minutes or until all the clams have opened. For extra richness, stir chilled butter into the sauce just before serving.
2. Ladle clams and sauce into serving bowls. Garnish with chopped herbs and freshly ground pepper and serve with a good crusty French bread. Provide an extra bowl for discarding empty shells.

meats

"The Market offers Vancouver shoppers looking for organic and seasonal produce an outstanding selection from which to choose. The bustling atmosphere and amazing array of specialty stores make shopping at the Market an experience, not a chore. Besides, the best hamburgers in town are at the Market Grill!"

—Rob Clark

THE BUTCHER'S TRADITION

In gentler times, an important part of the weekly shopping chores was a trip to the local butcher. You could chat with the person behind the counter, ask for special cuts, get tips on cooking or reserve hard-to-find cuts and products. The Market is one of the few places where that tradition is still alive and flourishing. The excellent butchers in the Market have built their reputations and businesses on making customer service a high priority. You can get a custom thickness or trim dressed right before your eyes. In these time-crunched days, the butchers here still offer meats that have been well aged, a process that enhances the flavour and tenderizes the meat. On the other hand, cognizant of the modern customer's desire for shortcuts, the butchers have developed many innovative, value-added products, including marinated and stuffed items that are ready for the oven, grill or fry pan with no preparation needed.

Beef: The Market is among the best places in the city to buy special cuts of beef. Osso bucco (sliced shank), prime rib, flank steak, organ meats and hard-to-find products such as caul fat are available from both of the butchers. Organic meats are gaining in popularity, and the price includes a premium for the expensive feed and low-volume processing. If you choose to buy organic, the Market merchants are dedicated to ensuring the products meet the strictest quality guidelines. Look for dull red flesh with a thin, creamy-yellow cap of fat and generous marbling.

Pork: Modern cuts of pork are much leaner than they were a few decades ago. Chops and ribs are ideal products for the barbecue. Shoulder, leg (including ham) and rib roasts are good for braising and roasting. Traditional thinking was that pork had to be well cooked to a uniform grey before many would consider it edible, but you can now safely consume pork when cooked through but still pink. (See the Cooking Temperature Chart on page 111 for a list of appropriate cooking temperatures.) Look for pale pink, firm meat with a firm, whitish fat layer. Greying fat indicates that the pork is less than fresh.

Lamb: Local lamb is available almost year round in our moderate climate. Imported American, Australian and New Zealand lamb also makes its way onto Market shelves. Ask the butcher about the origin of the lamb, and sample and compare to find the one you like best. Our preference is for the local, but you may feel differently depending on your liking for the slightly gamy taste of lamb. In general, lamb is being produced with leaner fat content and milder flavour. Lamb works wonderfully on the barbecue; just be sure to trim any excess fat to avoid flare-ups. The colour of the meat varies with the breed and feed of the lamb. Look for a whitish fat layer without any signs of yellowing. On a leg of lamb, the shin should be soft and pliable, not hard or cracked.

Game meats: Continually increasing in popularity, game meats are being farmed or ranged all across Canada. Imported products, particularly fallow venison from New Zealand, are also readily available. Game animals generally have a lower fat content and lower cholesterol count compared to domesticated pork or beef. Game meats are relatively new additions to our cultivated meat sources, so their gene pools have suffered little dilution through traditional animal husbandry techniques or modern genetic manipulation. Look for venison, rabbit, wild boar, goat, muskox and caribou. Ask your butcher for more details and cooking tips.

HOW TO GRILL A BEEFSTEAK

Serving individual steaks at a summer barbecue can be problematic. Individual appetites vary, and leftovers present a problem unless your guests admire an unusually high regimen of oral hygiene and are regular flossers. Besides, a big steak tastes better, and the "ooooh and ahhhh factor" when a Jurassic-sized piece of beef comes off the fire is worth the price of admission.

The Market butchers carry a good selection of Canada AAA beef. Call ahead to ensure that the beef has been aged (21 days minimum, 28 preferred) and that the right cut is available. You want a deep-cut sirloin, cut about 2¾ to 3 in/7 cm thick. Depending on the size of the animal, the cut will be about 3 to 3½ lbs/1.3 to 1.6 kg and will satisfy the cravings of about 6 of your lustiest friends. If you're really well organized and can plan well in advance, ask the butcher to order your beef from the Chutter Ranch in the Nicola Valley. Antibiotic and hormone-free, it tastes the way beef used to and still should. Chutter Ranch beef is available under the Ranchland brand.

Bank a charcoal grill with a hot fire to one side, a medium fire to the other. Real charcoal, which Canadian Tire usually carries, burns hotter and longer than briquettes. Alternatively, turn on your gas or propane grill, being sure to identify the location of cooler and hotter spots. (If you don't know where they are, try firing up in the dark to find out.)

About an hour before dinner, remove the steak from the refrigerator and bring it to room temperature. Just before grilling, dry the steak by blotting it with paper towel, then douse it on both sides with a good olive oil. Give the steak several generous grinds of salt and pepper, and place it on a platter. Skip the sugary barbecue sauces, which are meant for spareribs and which burn on a hot grill.

Oil the grill, either with paper towels or, better, with a mister. Place the steak on the hot section of the fire at an angle to the grill bars. After about 6 minutes, turn the steak 90 degrees and place it on the medium-hot section of the grill. (This results in beautiful cross-hatched grill marks.) Let it cook another 6 minutes or so, just until the juice begins to percolate to the top of the steak. Flip it with chef's tongs and repeat the process, again until you see juice on the surface, for a medium-rare steak.

Remove the steak to a clean platter or a carving board with a trough. Allow it to rest for at least 10 minutes. With a sharp knife, carve the steak against the grain and on an angle from top to bottom. Spoon the juices over the top and serve with hot horseradish.

Summertime grilling demands baked potatoes and corn (you can grill that too), but why limit yourself to fair weather? At cooler times of the year we serve grilled steak with scalloped potatoes and roasted young carrots and fennel, or with halves of roasted Bosc pears finished with a nugget of Gorgonzola cheese. Serve it with a well-aged Brunello to truly know bliss.

CINNAMON-CHILI RUBBED TEXAS FLANK STEAK

The intriguing addition of cinnamon makes this dish another aromatic winner. Make sure to cook the meat medium-rare and allow the steak to rest for at least as long as you cooked it. Chipotle paste is a dried and smoked chili that is available at South China Seas in cans, as whole chilies or in paste form. (Process whole peppers in a food processor to make a paste.)

Preparation time: Marinade, 2 hours or overnight; Steak, 20 minutes
Wine pairing: Merlot, Cabernet Sauvignon, Cabernet Franc

Serves 4

½ cup (125 mL) Mexican chili powder
1 tbsp (15 mL) ground cinnamon
salt and pepper to taste
2 lbs (900 g) flank steak, trimmed and scored
1 tbsp (15 mL) olive oil
½ cup (125 mL) beef stock
¼ cup (60 mL) honey
1 tbsp (15 mL) chipotle paste
1 tbsp (15 mL) unsalted butter

1. In a small bowl, combine chili powder, cinnamon, salt and pepper. Rub mixture on flank steak and refrigerate for a minimum of 2 hours (preferably 24 hours).
2. To a fry pan over high heat, add the olive oil and heat until very hot. Add the marinated steak and cook 3 to 4 minutes on each side. The meat should be rare at this stage. Remove meat from pan and let rest.
3. Add beef stock, honey and chipotle paste to the skillet over high heat. Reduce until thick enough to coat the back of a spoon. Whisk or swirl in the butter. Remove from heat and keep warm.
4. With a long, sharp knife, slice the flank steak thinly across the grain. Drizzle the sauce on and around the flank steak. Serve with mashed or pan-fried potatoes or rice and side vegetables.

GORDON MARTIN

Gordon Martin's earlier incarnation as a rock and roll musician may be the reason why his design instincts and vibrant creativity have been striking all the right chords on the Vancouver restaurant scene. Both Bin 941 (opened in June 1998) and Bin 942 (September 1999) are eclectically appointed, jazzy, high-energy, new world–style tapas and wine bars. Both rooms feature open frontages that, weather permitting, allow diners to enjoy the street scene outside while dining on plates brimming with variety and great taste. While training for his present role, Gord worked at some of Vancouver's finest restaurants, including the Century Grill, Raincity Grill, Allegro and the Wedgewood Hotel, but he credits his European travels for the birth of his passion.

"For so many years now, Granville Island has been a great place to shop. It is Vancouver's original market for farmers to bring their fresh, locally grown produce. It has always been a fun place to go, a place where you can bring the family and kids and enjoy spending the day shopping for Sunday night dinner."

—Robert Feenie

RED WINE–BRAISED BEEF RIBS

Use a nice-quality Merlot or Pinot Noir for this dish. The Stock Market is a good source of ready-made beef stock. The beef ribs improve in flavour if they are allowed to cool in the sauce and are then reheated prior to serving.
Preparation time: 2½ hours
Wine pairing: Merlot, Pinot Noir, Meritage

Serves 4

2 lbs (900 g) beef short ribs, trimmed and cut into 2 in/5 cm pieces
salt and pepper to taste
2 tbsp (30 mL) vegetable oil
1 medium yellow onion, finely chopped
3 cloves garlic, finely chopped
1 cup (250 mL) fruity red wine
2 cups (500 mL) rich veal or beef stock
3 whole fresh thyme sprigs
1 whole bay leaf

Oven: 300°F/150°C

1. Season ribs well with salt and pepper. In a heavy-bottomed roasting pan over medium-high heat, brown ribs in oil, about 5 to 7 minutes per side. Remove ribs and set aside. Remove all but 1 tbsp/15 mL of fat from the pan.
2. Reduce heat to medium and add onion and garlic. Cook uncovered for 2 minutes or until the onions begin to brown. Add wine and stir to deglaze the bottom of the pan. Add the stock, thyme, bay leaf and browned ribs. Bring to a boil, cover, and transfer pan to warm oven. Cook for 2 hours or until the meat falls off the bone. Turn meat occasionally.
3. Transfer ribs to a side plate and keep warm. Strain cooking liquid into a large saucepan and bring to a boil to reduce by half, about 10 minutes. Adjust seasonings. Place ribs in sauce and toss to coat evenly. Transfer to a serving bowl or platter. Serve with mashed potatoes and a side dish of garlic-sautéed greens.

ROBERT FEENIE

A native of Vancouver, Rob Feenie's tireless pursuit of culinary excellence has taken him to some of the finest kitchens across Europe and America. Time spent at legendary restaurants such as Au Crocodile and Le Beurehiesel with kitchen artists *par excellence* Emil Jung and Antoine Westermen formed the basis of Rob's impeccable classical technique and his creative cooking style. His elegant restaurant, Lumière, opened to instant critical success in 1995, and its reputation netted him an engagement as consultant to the prestigious Hotel Plaza Athenee in New York City. Not one to rest on his laurels, Rob is continuing to break new ground with his innovative menus featuring the best of local products. Lumière keeps winning awards as the top restaurant in Vancouver, proving bite after bite, year after year that he is not just a flash in the pan.

TEQUILA-MARINATED LAMB SKEWERS

with Goat Cheese Sauce

Try serving these tasty morsels to liven up a dinner party or as smaller, cocktail-size tidbits to fuel the fires of a crowd of people. As an alternative to grilling, the skewers can be pan-fried or baked in a hot oven until browned, transferred to a serving platter and drizzled with the sauce.

Preparation time: 45 minutes
Wine pairing: Cabernet Sauvignon, Merlot, Meritage

Serves 4

Lamb

¼ cup (60 mL) tequila
2 tbsp (30 mL) juniper berries, lightly crushed
4 tbsp (60 mL) olive oil
1 tsp (5 mL) rosemary, chopped
1 lb (450 g) lamb sirloin, well trimmed and sliced across the grain into 12 pieces
12 wooden skewers, soaked in water for 1 hour
salt and pepper to taste

Sauce

½ cup (125 mL) shallots, sliced
2 cups (500 mL) rich veal stock
¼ cup (60 mL) red wine
2 tbsp (30 mL) cold butter
¼ cup (60 mL) goat cheese, crumbled
Spiced Cornbread (see page 200)

Grill: hot

1. In a blender or food processor, combine the tequila, juniper berries, 3 tbsp/45 mL of the olive oil and the rosemary. Blend until a smooth purée is formed. Set aside to infuse flavours.
2. In a large bowl, combine the lamb slices with the marinade. Allow to rest in refrigerator for at least 2 hours to fully tenderize.
3. Thread the marinated lamb onto the soaked wooden skewers. Place in a nonreactive pan and pour marinade on top. Set aside.
4. In a saucepan over medium-high heat, add the remaining 1 tbsp/15 mL of oil and the shallots to the pan and sauté until the shallots are soft and begin to brown. Add the stock and red wine and cook until volume is reduced by half, about 10 minutes. Set aside.
5. Remove excess marinade from lamb skewers and season with salt and pepper. On a hot grill, cook skewers until browned and tender, about 2 minutes on each side.
6. Bring sauce just to a boil and whisk in the butter and goat cheese. Adjust seasoning to taste. To serve, place a piece of cornbread in the centre of each plate and top with 3 skewers of lamb. Spoon a portion of sauce on and around the skewers.

SEAN RILEY

A native of the West Coast, Sean was trained at Nanaimo's Malaspina College and went on to apprentice with Canadian Culinary Olympic Team captain Bruce Knapik at the Delta Hotel in Whistler. Working assignments followed at the CP Empress Hotel in Victoria and finally at the Metropolitan Hotel in Toronto, where Sean completed his training under Jack Lamont and superstar chef Susur Lee. Sean then worked with chef Emad Yacoub at Hogan's Inn before returning with Yacoub to Vancouver to take over the stoves of Vancouver's popular Joe Fortes Restaurant. At Brix, a relatively new wine bar offering regular and tapas menus, Sean is becoming known for his exciting presentations and intense flavours. A regular Market shopper, Sean likes to make use of exotic grains and vegetables and praises the merchants for their service and attention to detail.

GRILLED PORK RIBS

with Spicy Plum Glaze

Grilling ribs is a summertime ritual that takes us back to our primitive roots. There is something deeply satisfying about eating these morsels with your hands. It is useful to have a small bowl filled with warm water and a slice of lemon (to cut the grease), along with plenty of paper towels. You can make your own plum sauce by stewing fresh fruit with a small quantity of water and sugar to taste. These ribs can also be successfully roasted or broiled in an oven.

Preparation time: 45 minutes
Wine pairing: Ehrenfelser, full-bodied Chardonnay, fruity Gamay

Serves 4 to 6

Ribs

4 lbs (1.8 kg) pork back or side ribs, trimmed and cut into 6 in/15 cm pieces
4 ginger slices
2 tbsp (30 mL) olive oil
salt and pepper to taste

Glaze

1 cup (250 mL) commercial plum sauce
juice and zest of 1 lime
1 tbsp (15 mL) fresh ginger, shredded
1 tbsp (15 mL) chili paste

Grill: medium-hot

1. To a large pot filled with boiling, salted water, add the ribs and ginger. Return to a boil, reduce heat and simmer for 20 minutes. Drain ribs, discard water and allow ribs to cool and dry slightly. Place in a low-sided pan and season with olive oil, salt and pepper. Toss until the ribs are evenly coated; set aside. (The ribs may be cooked in advance and refrigerated at this point.)
2. In a saucepan over medium-high heat, combine the plum sauce, lime juice and zest, ginger and chili paste. Stir until melted and remove from heat. Set aside.
3. On a hot grill, cook ribs until browned and crisp on the surface, about 5 minutes per side. Brush with sauce, flip on grill and cook until ribs are slightly charred. Brush with additional sauce and transfer to platter. Cut ribs into individual pieces by running a knife between the bones. Baste with a final coating of sauce and serve warm.

TIPS ON GRILLING

Always preheat grill to desired temperature before starting. If grilling marinated meats, brush off excess marinade, pat dry, if possible, and lightly brush ingredients with oil before placing on grill. Be patient; allow ingredients to remain on the grill long enough to be well marked before attempting to turn and to prevent sticking. For thicker cuts of meats, mark well and finish cooking in a heated oven, then allow to rest off the heat for a few minutes before cutting or slicing. Keep a spray bottle of water on hand. If the grill flares up, simply douse the flames with a squirt of water.

BAKED PORK CHOPS
with Mushroom-Mustard Sauce

For an equally delicious, kid-friendly version of this recipe, omit the mushrooms and replace the mustard with ½ cup/125 mL of applesauce and a squeeze of lemon. Alternatively, instead of applesauce, add 1 large, peeled, cored and thinly sliced apple to the sauce and cook for 3 minutes or until apple is soft.

Preparation time: 40 minutes
Wine pairing: Pinot Noir, Cabernet Franc, full-bodied Chardonnay

Serves 4

4 centre-cut loin pork chops, about 1 in/2.5 cm thick
1 tsp (5 mL) seasoned salt (or to taste)
freshly ground black pepper
2 tbsp (30 mL) olive oil
1 cup (250 mL) onions, sliced
2 cups (500 mL) cremini mushrooms, sliced
¼ cup (60 mL) medium sherry
½ cup (125 mL) chicken or veal stock
1 tbsp (15 mL) Dijon mustard (or to taste)
1 tbsp (15 mL) parsley, chopped, for garnish

Oven: 400°F/200°C

1. Season both sides of pork chops well with seasoned salt and pepper. To a large, heavy ovenproof skillet or fry pan over high heat, add oil and heat until very hot. Add pork chops and sear until golden brown, about 2 minutes on each side. Remove chops and set aside on a plate.
2. Add onions and mushrooms to skillet and stir-fry until vegetables are soft and lightly brown, about 1 to 2 minutes. Add sherry and cook for 1 minute.
3. Return pork chops and juices to skillet; add stock, stir and cover. Place in oven and cook for 20 minutes or until chops are tender, turning the chops once or twice during cooking.
4. Transfer pork chops to serving platter, leaving mushroom sauce mixture in skillet. Bring sauce to boil over medium-high heat. Add mustard; stir and bring to boil. Taste and adjust seasonings. Pour sauce over pork chops. Garnish with a sprinkle of parsley and serve.

poultry

CRISPY ROASTED CHICKEN WITH
CHILI, LIME AND GARLIC

ZESTY CHICKEN BROCHETTES WITH LEMON SALSA

PHEASANT BRAISED IN ROSEMARY AND FRUIT JUICE

TURKEY STUFFED WITH WILD MUSHROOM POLENTA

ASIAN BARBECUED DUCK QUESADILLAS

LAVENDER-HONEY DUCK BREAST WITH
BANYULS SAUCE

-FR
Speci
often call
- chemica
- grain di
- air chill
$4.39 lb.

"We live just across False Creek from the Market, so we often pack up the kids, cutting boards, knives and condiments and spend the day at the water park or just roaming around the Market area. If you have to do some serious shopping, get to the Market early. You can start shopping even before the Market officially opens."

—Daryle Nagata

HOME ON THE FREE RANGE

On any given day in the Market, you can find quality Grade A, organic or free-range chicken, turkey, duck, goose, quail, guinea fowl and Cornish game hen. For the best results, buy fresh, unfrozen poultry. Pound for pound, organic and free-range birds will provide better flavour. Poultry should be stored (tightly wrapped) in the refrigerator and used within one to two days of purchase. Make a special effort to keep the poultry from cross-contaminating other foods in your refrigerator, particularly foods that will be eaten raw (such as vegetables).

Chicken: Chicken is probably the most inexpensive and popular poultry product on the market today. Having said that, for superior texture and flavour, we recommend that you pay a bit more and try the free-range and specialty chicken that is available in the Market. The popularity of chicken, however, may also have spawned its somewhat ill-deserved reputation as a common cause of salmonella poisoning. To be safe, avoid chicken with off-putting odours; store chicken in the coldest part of the fridge; wash and sanitize utensils and surfaces after cutting chicken; and cook until the juices run clear from the thickest part of the thigh. (See Cooking Temperature Chart, page 225.)

Duck: The succulent, tasty dark meat of duck has elevated it to many festive tables. Local ducks, most notably from the Fraser Valley, are available year-round and are reputed to be descended from the Chinese brood stock. When buying fresh duck, look for plump, unblemished skin; the freshest duck has a soft and pliable skin. Duck is best used within one to two days but will keep up to three days if well wrapped and refrigerated. Frozen duck should come in a vacuum-sealed package and the skin should be free of frostbite (dry, white patches). Defrost slowly in the refrigerator for the best results. Modern chefs are fond of cooking duck breasts and legs separately, as the legs can be a bit sinewy and often require slow-cooking treatment such as roasting or slow poaching in oil.

Goose: Making a comeback in the local market, goose can be excellent when roasted or braised to eliminate the considerable fat content. Young geese have a mild and luxurious flavour and are usually quite tender. Older birds can become tough and are usually suitable only for braising and moist-heat cooking. Look for a small bird, less than 9 lbs/4 kg for the best results, and choose a bird with clean, whitish skin that is smooth and dry to the touch.

Turkey: Fresh turkeys have superior flavour, moistness and tenderness when compared to frozen ones. The flesh should be firm, plump and dry to the touch. Free-range turkeys often have smaller breasts and a greater proportion of lean, dark meat. Recently, wild turkeys have been cultivated on local farms and occasionally appear in the Market, usually around the major fall and Christmas holidays. These birds are smaller and leaner but are packed with true turkey flavour. The small size is perfect for a couple who wants to celebrate with a turkey without having to live with a mountain of leftovers.

Specialty birds: Careful trolling through the aisles of the Market will yield a wealth of specialty poultry options. Quail is increasing in popularity, the small size making a great appetizer. One quail, stuffed, or two, grilled, roasted or pan-fried, will make a great meal per person. Silky chickens are a black-skinned Chinese variety, renowned as soup or stew chickens. Guinea fowl are beautifully plumed birds that are very lean and flavourful. Pheasants are famous for their dark breast meat and the rich texture and flavour of their flesh.

CRISPY ROASTED CHICKEN WITH CHILI, LIME AND GARLIC

Splitting the chicken in half helps speed up the cooking time of this simple dish. The chicken is flattened onto a roasting pan, exposing all of the skin. The lime juice helps render the skin very crispy and gives it a spicy, tangy bite.

Preparation time: 1¼ hours
Wine pairing: Gamay, Pinot Meunier

Serves 4

1 roasting chicken (about 3 lbs/1.3 kg)
1 tbsp (15 mL) olive oil
salt and pepper to taste
2 tbsp (30 mL) garlic, minced
1 tsp (5 mL) ancho chili, ground, or chili powder
1 tsp (5 mL) cayenne pepper
1 tsp (5 mL) paprika
zest and juice of 1 lime

Oven: 400°F/200°C

1. On a flat work surface, lay the chicken breast-side down. With a sharp knife (or kitchen scissors), cut along the back of the chicken into the cavity. Pull apart the sides and flatten the chicken with your hands.
2. Place chicken in a heavy roasting pan or ovenproof skillet. Drizzle with oil and rub chicken with hands to evenly coat the skin. Season both sides well with salt and pepper. Rub the minced garlic on the underside of the bird and place cavity-side down in the pan. Sprinkle skin with ancho chili, cayenne pepper, paprika and lime zest. Squeeze lime juice over the chicken and allow to sit for at least 10 minutes.
3. Place in oven and roast until skin is crisp and golden brown, about 1 hour. Let sit for at least 10 minutes before serving.

ZESTY CHICKEN BROCHETTES

with Lemon Salsa

Serve these tasty, quick-and-easy chicken skewers with mesclun greens for lunch or with mashed potatoes and vegetables for dinner. The same marinade works very well with prawns, salmon, halibut and even pork chops. You can make this dish under a hot broiler if a grill is not available.

Preparation time: 40 minutes
Wine pairing: Riesling, Chenin Blanc

Serves 4

Salsa

- 1 whole lemon, finely chopped
- 1 medium Spanish onion, finely chopped
- 2 tbsp (30 mL) olive oil
- ½ cup (125 mL) parsley, chopped
- 1 tbsp (15 mL) honey (or to taste)
- salt and freshly ground pepper

Chicken

- 8 boneless, skinless chicken thighs, each cut into quarters
- 1 cup (250 mL) coconut milk
- 2 tbsp (30 mL) mango chutney
- 2 tbsp (30 mL) fish sauce
- 2 tbsp (30 mL) finely chopped cilantro stems and roots if available
- 1 tsp (5 mL) dried chili flakes (or to taste)
- 8 wooden skewers, soaked in water for 30 minutes

Oven: 250ºF/120ºC

1. In a deep ovenproof skillet or Dutch oven, heat oil over medium-high heat. Season pheasant with salt and pepper and fry until well browned, about 4 to 5 minutes per side.
2. Drain excess fat from pan and add the rosemary and orange, pineapple and apple juices. Bring to a boil, transfer to a warm oven and braise for 1½ to 2 hours or until meat is tender and almost falls off the bones.
3. With a slotted spoon, remove the pheasant from the sauce and transfer to a serving plate. Cover with aluminum foil and keep warm. Reduce braising liquid by half, or to a sauce consistency. Adjust seasonings with salt and pepper and pour sauce over the pheasant. Serve warm, accompanied with steamed vegetables and rice.

ROBERT BULLER

With his love for food, Robert might have become a chef; instead he chose a career in marketing and business and spent time as a business instructor at Queen's University in Kingston. Today he owns a shop that sells organic and specialty poultry in the Public Market and is a busy member of Vancouver's Planning Commission. An affable fellow who seems to vibrate with endless energy, Robert is constantly in pursuit of new ideas and products to bring to market. Working closely with chef Jan Riggs, Robert has developed an ever-expanding collection of new dishes and value-added products for the store and its burgeoning catering service.

TURKEY STUFFED WITH WILD MUSHROOM POLENTA

Polenta is dense, moist and rich. The wild mushrooms add an earthy and savoury flavour and absorb all the delicious juices. Be sure to remove all stuffing from the leftover turkey and store it separately. You can mould the leftover stuffing into little pancakes and pan-fry them until crisp for a delicious second meal.

Preparation time: 4 to 5 hours
(Cook turkey for 15 to 20 minutes per lb/30 to 40 minutes per kg)

Wine pairing: Pinot Noir, Cabernet Franc, Gamay

Serves 6 to 8

Stuffing

4 cups (1 L) water
1 tbsp (15 mL) salt
2 cups (500 mL) cornmeal
4 slices smoked bacon, diced (optional) or 2 tbsp/30 mL oil
2 cups (500 mL) leeks, sliced
2 tbsp (30 mL) garlic, minced
1 lb (450 g) wild mushrooms, chopped (chanterelle, pine, cauliflower, black trumpet, porcini)
3 tbsp (45 mL) sage, minced

Turkey

1 turkey (15 lbs/6.75 kg)
sea salt and pepper
2 tbsp (30 mL) olive oil
2 carrots, peeled and chopped
2 medium onions, chopped
2 celery stalks, chopped
2 cups (500 mL) apple cider or white wine

Gravy

3 tbsp (45 mL) flour
8 cups (2 L) turkey or chicken stock, warmed

Oven: 325°F/160°C

1. In a large, heavy-bottomed saucepan, bring the water and salt to a boil. Add the cornmeal and stir well to mix. Cook for 5 minutes, stirring constantly, until the polenta is thick and soft to the bite. Pour into a buttered baking tray and cool.
2. In a large fry pan over medium-high heat, fry the bacon until crisp (or warm the oil). Reduce heat to medium and add leeks, garlic, mushrooms and sage. Sauté until all vegetables are soft, about 5 minutes. Transfer to a large bowl. Cut the cooled polenta into small cubes and add to the mushroom mixture. Toss well to coat and work with hands until a smooth mass is formed.
3. Wash the turkey under cold water and pat dry with paper towels. Season the inside cavity with salt and pepper. Stuff the turkey with the polenta mixture. Drizzle olive oil over the turkey and rub into the skin; season outside with salt and pepper.
4. Place the carrots, onions and celery in a large, deep roasting pan. Pour cider over the vegetables. Place turkey on top of vegetables and roast for about 3½ hours. If the skin browns too quickly, cover with a piece of aluminum foil. Add more liquid if the pan becomes dry. The turkey is done when a meat thermometer inserted into the thigh registers 180°F/82°C. The drumstick will twist easily and the juices will run clear.
5. Remove bird from oven and transfer to a large platter; let sit for at least 15 minutes. Meanwhile, place the roasting pan on the stove over medium-high heat and reduce the liquid. When the moisture has almost evaporated and the solids begin to brown, sprinkle the flour into the pan and stir with a wooden spoon to mix with the pan juices. If the mixture is too wet, add a little more flour to form a thick paste.
6. Add a little stock to the pan and whisk until a smooth paste is formed. Gradually add stock until the mixture is smooth and thin. Heat until bubbling and whisk the gravy to break up any lumps of vegetables. Reduce heat, season with salt and pepper and simmer for 10 minutes. Strain with a coarse sieve and reserve. Thin with additional stock if necessary.
7. Carve the turkey into white and dark slices. Serve with gravy, vegetables and mashed potatoes.

ASIAN BARBECUED DUCK QUESADILLAS

Buying duck at a Chinese barbecue store will quickly speed up the time it takes to get dinner on the table. Substitute cooked chicken or turkey for the duck with excellent results.

Preparation time: 20 minutes
Wine pairing: Full-bodied Riesling, fruity sparkling wine

Serves 4

1 tbsp (15 mL) butter
1 tsp (5 mL) sesame oil
1 cup (250 mL) red and yellow peppers, thinly sliced
½ cup (125 mL) broccoli, thinly sliced
4 10 in/25 cm flour tortillas
1 cup (250 mL) boneless barbecued duck, sliced
½ cup (125 mL) pressed tofu, thinly sliced
1 cup (250 mL) soy cheese
¼ cup (60 mL) green onions, sliced
2 tbsp (30 mL) vegetable oil
¼ cup (60 mL) hoisin sauce, thinned with a little boiling water
2 tbsp (30 mL) sesame seeds

HOISIN SAUCE

A Chinese condiment made from a combination of fermented soybean and yam, flavoured with spices and sugar, hoisin sauce provides a rich base for stir-fries and dressings and is wonderful on Peking duck rolls.

Oven: warm

1. In a nonstick fry pan over medium-high heat, heat butter and sesame oil. Sauté peppers and broccoli for 2 minutes or until vegetables are tender.
2. To make the quesadillas, place two of the tortillas on a flat work surface. Sprinkle the duck, tofu, soy cheese, green onions and cooked vegetables evenly over top. Top each with a second tortilla, pressing down gently.
3. In a large nonstick fry pan over medium heat, heat 1 tbsp/15 mL of the oil and gently place 1 quesadilla in the pan. Brown on both sides, about 2 minutes per side. Transfer to a warm oven while you repeat the process with the other quesadilla. Place on a cutting board and cut each into 12 wedges. Drizzle with hoisin sauce, sprinkle with sesame seeds and serve.

DARYLE NAGATA

Alberta-born chef Daryle Nagata has roamed the world, cooking for kings, queens and presidents along the way. His professional culinary explorations have taken him to London, England's Savoy and Hilton Park Lane hotels and Switzerland's Hotel La Reserve. Daryle is a proud Canadian who actively supports our cuisine and culture. When he can tear himself away from his full schedule at the CP Waterfront Centre Hotel, Daryle loves to bring his family to the Market. His favourite meals are family-style picnics with fresh greens, vegetables, breads, pâté, cold cuts, seafood and, of course, fresh fruit and berries for dessert.

LAVENDER-HONEY DUCK BREAST

with Banyuls Sauce

This dish showcases Dino's command of flavour and technique. It cries out for a great bottle of Pinot Noir. Serve with a side dish of steamed or sautéed cabbage and mashed or roasted potatoes.

Preparation time: 30 minutes
Wine pairing: Pinot Noir, Merlot, Pinot Meunier

Serves 4

Duck

4 duck breasts
4 shallots, minced
1 cup (250 mL) white wine
½ tsp (2.5 mL) dry mustard
1 tsp (5 mL) garlic, minced
2 bay leaves
1 tbsp (15 mL) thyme, chopped
1 tbsp (15 mL) lavender leaves, chopped
2 tbsp (30 mL) wildflower honey
freshly ground pepper

Sauce

1 cup (250 mL) Banyuls wine or port
2 cups (500 mL) rich duck or veal stock
salt and pepper
1 tbsp (15 mL) cold butter
lavender or rosemary sprigs for garnish

1. Trim duck breasts of any excess fat. With a sharp knife, make a few shallow cuts in the duck skin along the length of each breast (be careful not to cut through skin). Turn at a 45-degree angle and repeat to form a cross-hatch pattern. Repeat with each breast.
2. In a nonreactive bowl, combine shallots, wine, mustard, garlic, bay leaves, thyme, lavender, honey and a grinding of fresh pepper. Add duck breasts, turning to coat. Marinate in the refrigerator for at least 2 hours or overnight, turning occasionally. Before making sauce, drain duck breasts well and reserve marinade.
3. In a medium saucepan over high heat, bring Banyuls wine to boil and cook until volume is reduced by half. Add stock and reserved marinade and cook to reduce to one-third the original volume. It should have the consistency of a thin sauce that coats the back of a spoon. Set aside.
4. To a large nonstick fry pan over medium-high heat, add the duck, skin-side down, and season with salt and pepper. When the duck starts to sizzle, reduce heat to medium and cook for about 10 minutes, or until the fat is rendered and the skin is crispy and deep golden brown. Turn over and cook meat-side down for about 5 minutes. Remove from heat and let duck rest for 2 to 3 minutes.
5. Meanwhile, bring sauce back to boil over high heat. Remove from heat and whisk in the cold butter. Season with salt and pepper.
6. To serve, spoon sauce onto warmed plates. Slice each duck breast into thin slices and fan on top of the sauce. Garnish plate with a sprig of lavender or rosemary. Accompany with mashed or roasted potatoes and vegetables.

seafood

ROASTED SALMON WITH YELLOW TOMATOES, MARJORAM AND GARLIC

HERB-CRUSTED HALIBUT WITH MUSHROOM-SPINACH RAGOUT

CUMIN SWORDFISH WITH GRILLED ASPARAGUS SALSA

PAN-FRIED TROUT WITH HERB BROTH

CORIANDER-CRUSTED TUNA WITH CHERRY TOMATOES AND GREEN PEPPERCORNS

PAN-SEARED LING COD WITH PRUNE-PLUM SAUCE

GRILLED PRAWNS WITH SPICY PEACH SALSA

GRILLED SQUID WITH APPLE-MANGO VINAIGRETTE

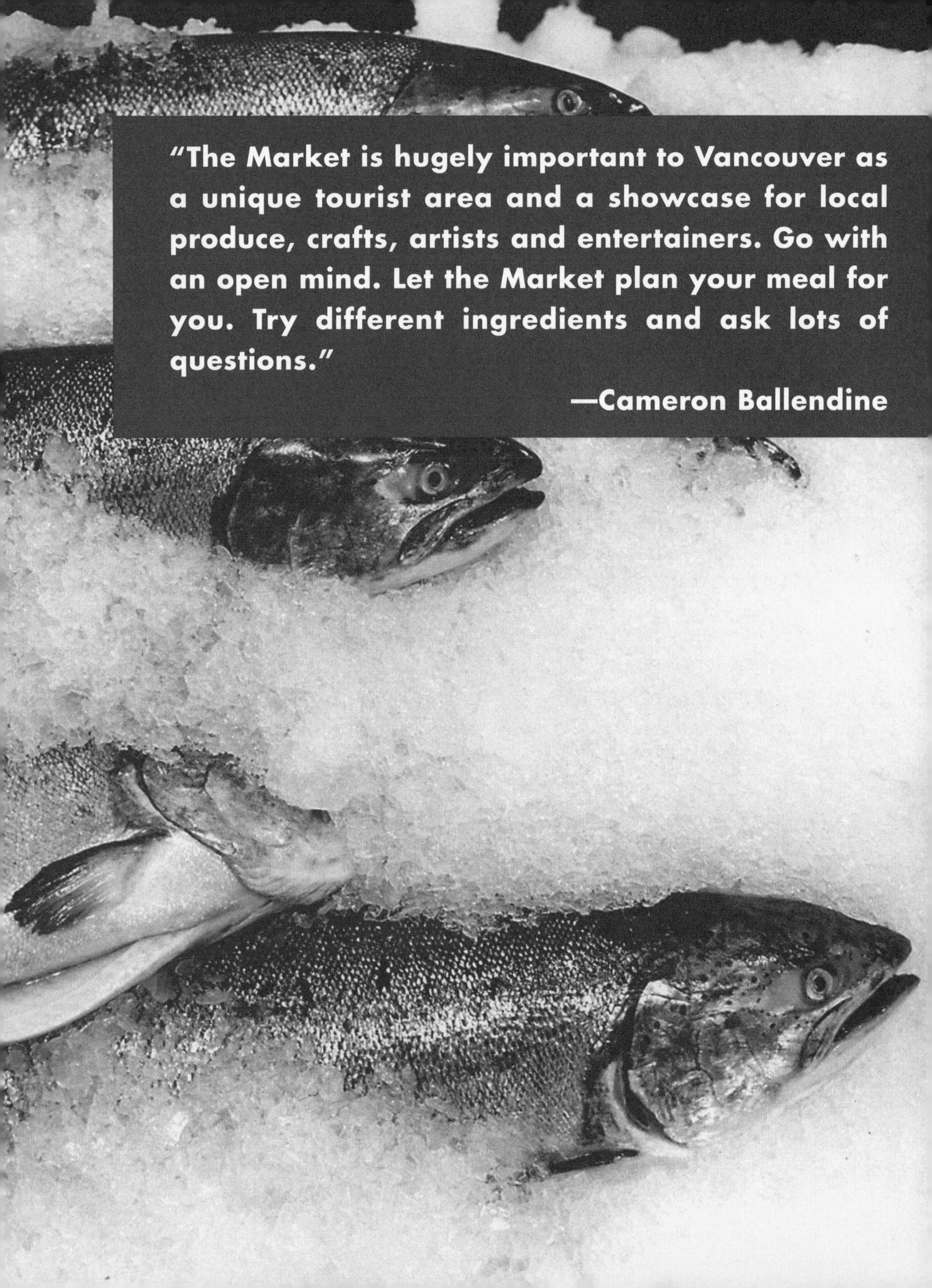
"The Market is hugely important to Vancouver as a unique tourist area and a showcase for local produce, crafts, artists and entertainers. Go with an open mind. Let the Market plan your meal for you. Try different ingredients and ask lots of questions."
—Cameron Ballendine

FISH BUYING TIPS

There is no more compelling argument for the superiority of shopping at the Market than the gleaming rows of whole fish laid on mounds of crushed ice. The quality and freshness of the Market seafood is legendary and firmly etched in the minds of tourists and locals alike. The merchants take great pride in their fish and have set very high standards. In general, fresh seafood should smell as sweet as the ocean it came from. A pronounced fishy smell usually means the fish has declined past its prime. Fresh fish will have bright red gills and clear, not sunken, eyes. When prodded, the flesh of the fish should be plump and spring back to the touch. Avoid frozen fish that has been thawed unless it meets the freshness criteria stated above. Frozen fish and shellfish should be properly glazed and frozen and free of frost burn (dry, milky coloured flesh). If the fish has been frozen at sea, the quality can often be superior to fresh fish that has been mistreated. Cleaning fish is off-putting to many people, and the merchants will be happy to slice or prepare your fish to your requirements.

Salmon: These gleaming ocean-travelling, freshwater, spawning fish are a coveted treasure in British Columbia, both gastronomically and psychologically. The six unique species of West Coast wild salmon are chinook (king or spring), coho (silver), sockeye (red), chum (silverbright or keta), pink (humpie) and steelhead trout (these ocean-migrating rainbow trout are now considered part of the salmon family). Locally farmed, fresh Atlantic and chinook salmon are available year–round as well. Troll-caught salmon are individually landed (not caught in a net), resulting in high-quality fish, and command a much higher price.

Halibut: Pacific halibut is one of the finest-tasting fish available on the West Coast. With the implementation of the quota system, it is now available fresh year-round, although the supply can be low. Its large size and thick skin make halibut quite hardy, and it retains its optimal quality very well even when frozen. It is best when cooked through until the fish is just firm. If overcooked it has a tendency to become a bit dry. Halibut cheeks are considered a delicacy and can weigh up to 6 oz/170 g in some of the bigger fish. (The largest halibut can easily exceed 500 lbs/225 kg.) When buying halibut, look for pieces that are plump, firm and shiny. Older fish will look mushy and tend to break into segments.

Tuna: The vast majority of tuna in the Market comes from the tropical waters of Hawaii and equatorial parts of the Pacific Ocean. Ahi tuna is the Hawaiian name for two main varieties: yellowfin and bigeye tuna. Both species have deep red flesh and are prized as the ultimate sushi fish. Ahi should be grilled medium-rare, like beef, to preserve the wonderful texture and meaty flavour. Locally, albacore tuna is fished in the cool water off the Pacific coast. Traditionally the majority of albacore was converted into canned tuna. Fresh albacore is now commonly available in the Market. The smaller loins are perfect for the barbecue.

Other fin fish: For an exploration of local seafood, look in the Market for lesser-known fish. We recommend you seek out ling cod, sablefish (black cod or butterfish), rockfish (snapper, China, yelloweye, canary, quillback, et cetera), skate, mackerel, Pacific sole and cabezon. Freshwater fish including rainbow trout, Arctic char, catfish, tilapia and carp are also available from time to time.

ROASTED SALMON

with Yellow Tomatoes, Marjoram and Garlic

Roasting the tomatoes in a hot oven renders them into a sweet and intense topping. Use a full-flavoured salmon such as sockeye or spring for the best results.

Preparation time: 20 minutes
Wine pairing: Pinot Gris, light fruity Pinot Noir

Serves 4

4 salmon fillets, 6 oz/170 g each
2 large yellow or red tomatoes, thinly sliced
1 tbsp (15 mL) marjoram, minced
1 tsp (5 mL) garlic, minced
1 tbsp (15 mL) extra-virgin olive oil
salt and pepper

Oven: 400°F/200°C

1. Place the fillets on a baking sheet lined with parchment paper. Top each with the tomato slices. Sprinkle with marjoram, garlic, olive oil, salt and pepper.
2. Roast for 10 minutes or until the tomatoes are slightly dry and the salmon flesh is firm and beginning to brown on the bottom.
3. Remove from oven and serve with steamed new potatoes tossed with butter and chives and a side dish of steamed broccoli or cauliflower.

JANICE KARIOTAKIS

Janice and Drake Kouriastakis have been serving their loyal customers since the early days of the Market. The Salmon Shop's logo of a leaping salmon has become the symbol of quality seafood and friendly, helpful service for a generation of Vancouverites. Whether you're looking for a whole salmon packaged to travel or a fillet of marinated swordfish for a quick dinner, Janice and her staff are ready to deliver with a smile. Janice, a great supporter of the *Chefs in the Market* program, is also a great cook with a special place in her heart for, you guessed it, salmon.

cameron ballendine

RESTAURANT CHEF, THE CREEK RESTAURANT, BREWERY & LOUNGE

HERB-CRUSTED HALIBUT

with Mushroom-Spinach Ragout

The bread crumb coating is a crusty exterior that guarantees a very moist interior. Panko are Japanese-style bread crumbs that are available in the Market at South China Seas. You can, if you wish, substitute stale white bread (crusts removed), shredded with a cheese grater. Reduce a strong veal stock to one-quarter of the original volume to make your own demi-glace. The Stock Market carries a line of fine premade stocks.

Preparation time: 30 minutes
Wine pairing: Sauvignon Blanc, Semillon, lightly oaked Pinot Gris or Kerner

Serves 4

Halibut

4 halibut fillets, 6 oz/170 g each
salt and pepper
3 tbsp (45 mL) olive oil
¼ cup (60 mL) mixed herbs, finely chopped (parsley, chives, dill, chervil, etc.)
¼ cup (60 mL) panko (white bread crumbs)

Ragout

4 shallots, peeled and minced
½ lb (225 g) shiitake mushrooms
½ lb (225 g) oyster mushrooms
½ cup (125 mL) white wine
¼ cup (60 mL) veal demi-glace or stock
½ lb (225 g) baby spinach leaves, washed and trimmed

Oven: 400°F/200°C

1. Season halibut with salt, pepper and 1 tbsp/15 mL of the olive oil. Rub fish to evenly distribute the seasoning. In a shallow dish, combine herbs and panko, stirring well to mix. Roll the fish in the bread crumb mixture.
2. To an ovenproof fry pan over medium-high heat, add 1 tbsp/5 mL of the olive oil and heat until hot. Add the halibut and fry for 1 to 2 minutes per side to sear. Place in a hot oven and bake for 7 to 8 minutes. Remove from oven and allow to rest for 3 to 4 minutes.
3. Meanwhile, prepare the ragout. In a large nonstick fry pan over medium-high heat, add remaining olive oil and heat until hot. Add the shallots and mushrooms and stir-fry for 2 to 3 minutes or until the mushrooms begin to soften. Add the wine and reduce until almost all the moisture is evaporated, about 5 to 6 minutes. Add the demi-glace and reduce until it thickens and coats the back of a spoon. Season with salt and pepper.
4. Stir in spinach and allow to wilt in the sauce, about 1 minute. Serve with mashed potatoes topped with a fillet of halibut. Spoon the ragout around and over the fish.

CAMERON BALLENDINE

A local boy, Cameron began his cooking career at Nanaimo's Malaspina College and continued to hone his craft at illustrious restaurants across western Canada. His impressive résumé lists Vancouver's Pan Pacific Hotel, Calgary's Delta Bow Valley and Canadian Pacific's Empress, Chateau Whistler and Chateau Lake Louise properties. Currently presiding over the stoves at The Creek, Cameron continues to travel the world for culinary competitions and pleasure when his schedule permits. His favourite meal is Market-fresh and simple: a fresh baguette, some ripe cheese, crisp grapes and a big fruity wine from the Okanagan Valley. "It doesn't get any better than that!" he exclaims.

CUMIN SWORDFISH
with Grilled Asparagus Salsa

This was probably one of the best-received recipes served in our cooking series. The audience loved the fragrant smell of toasting cumin, and the seared swordfish was extremely tender and juicy.

Preparation time: 30 minutes
Wine pairing: Semillon, Sauvignon Blanc, Gamay

Serves 4

Salsa

1 lb (450 g) asparagus, peeled and trimmed
1 red onion, peeled and quartered
1 red pepper, quartered and seeded
3 jalapeño peppers, halved and seeded
1 tbsp (15 mL) garlic, minced
1 tbsp (15 mL) olive oil
salt and pepper
juice of 3 limes
2 tbsp (30 mL) mirin (Japanese rice wine) or 1 tsp (5 mL) honey
2 tbsp (30 mL) chili oil (or to taste)

Swordfish

1 tbsp (15 mL) ground cumin
1 tsp (5 mL) ground coriander
salt and pepper
4 swordfish steaks, 6 oz/170 g each
1 tbsp (15 mL) olive oil
4 cups (1 L) rice, freshly cooked
basil for garnish

Grill: hot

1. In a mixing bowl, combine the asparagus, onion, red pepper, jalapeño peppers, garlic and olive oil. Toss to coat and season well with salt and pepper. On hot, oiled grill, cook the asparagus until slightly charred and soft, about 5 minutes. Set aside to cool.
2. Dice vegetables and return to the bowl. Season with lime juice, mirin and chili oil. Season lightly with salt and pepper and set aside.
3. In a small bowl, combine cumin, coriander, salt and pepper. Place the swordfish on a plate and sprinkle both sides with the spice mixture.
4. To a nonstick fry pan over medium-high heat, add the olive oil. When hot, sear the swordfish on each side for 4 to 5 minutes or until golden brown. Transfer to a plate and keep warm.
5. To serve, place a heaping pile of rice on a plate; top with a fillet of swordfish and spoon one-quarter of the salsa mixture over one corner of the fish. Garnish with a sprig of basil.

ASPARAGUS

When buying asparagus, pick stalks that are firm, bright green and have tight tips that are not dried out or wilted. White asparagus, a rare treat, should be plump and smooth skinned. Choose spears no thicker than your little finger for sautés and salads; thicker ones can be very good braised. Peel the base of fibrous stalks or trim them and use them for soup. Asparagus will store quite well wrapped loosely in a plastic bag for three to five days. Look for local asparagus in the Market between May and June. Asparagus is a good source of vitamin A and contains a fair amount of iron and vitamins B and C.

PAN-FRIED TROUT
with Herb Broth

The perfect trout for pan-frying is about 1 lb/450 g. Fresh trout will have pink gills and a thin coating of slime. Rainbow, steelhead and Arctic char all work well in this recipe.

Preparation time: 25 minutes
Wine pairing: Pinot Blanc, Pinot Gris, dry Bacchus

Serves 4

Broth

- 2 cups (500 mL) fish stock
- 1 tsp (5 mL) white wine vinegar
- ¼ cup (60 mL) extra-virgin olive oil
- 2 tbsp (30 mL) thyme, chopped
- 2 tbsp (30 mL) rosemary, chopped
- salt and pepper
- 1 tbsp (15 mL) butter

Trout

- ½ cup (125 mL) flour
- 1 tsp (5 mL) thyme, finely chopped
- 1 tsp (5 mL) rosemary, finely chopped
- salt and pepper
- 4 trout, 1 lb/450 g each, cleaned and rinsed
- 2 tbsp (30 mL) olive oil
- 1 tbsp (15 mL) butter

Oven: warm

1. To make the broth, in a medium saucepan over high heat combine the fish stock, vinegar and olive oil. Bring to a boil, reduce heat and simmer for 2 minutes. Remove from heat and stir in thyme and rosemary. Season with salt and pepper and allow to sit for at least 5 minutes to infuse flavours.
2. On a plate, combine flour, thyme, rosemary, salt and pepper and mix well. Dredge trout in the seasoned flour to evenly coat the skin.
3. In a large, cast-iron fry pan over medium-high heat, warm the oil and 1 tbsp/15 mL butter. When the butter begins to sizzle, fry the trout and season again with salt and pepper. Reduce heat to medium and cook each side until golden brown, about 5 minutes per side. Transfer to a warm oven while finishing the sauce.
4. Return the fish broth to medium heat and bring to a simmer. Remove from heat and whisk in the butter. To serve, divide trout among 4 warmed plates and top each with the herb broth.

ROMY PRASAD

Growing up in Guyana, Romy Prasad had his appreciation for fine food nurtured by his mother, who ground spices by hand and prepared the family's meals on a wood-fired stove. Sparked by the energy of the restaurant business while working his way through university, Romy enrolled in Ontario's well-known Stratford Chef School and later attended the Ritz Escoffier Cooking School in Paris. His search for culinary excellence also took him to restaurants such as Pierre Ganier in Saint-Ettiene, France; Arzak in San Sebastian, Spain; Al Cantuccio in Arona, Italy; and the Quilted Giraffe in New York City. Currently, Romy has settled in comfortably as chef at the award-winning CinCin Ristorante on Robson Street. On those rare occasions when he can get away, Romy can be found hiking in the local mountains or exploring Vancouver, which of course includes strolling through the Public Market.

CORIANDER-CRUSTED TUNA

with Cherry Tomatoes and Green Peppercorns

Dennis uses the best ahi tuna available. It's usually labelled "sushi grade" and is a premium product, caught and processed under the strictest of standards.

Preparation time: 20 minutes
Wine pairing: Pinot Noir, full-bodied Blanc de Noir sparkling wine

Serves 4

2 shallots, finely minced
2 tbsp (30 mL) olive oil
juice and zest of 1 lemon
1 tsp (5 mL) coarse salt
1 tbsp (15 mL) green peppercorns in brine
2 cups (500 mL) cherry tomatoes, halved
1 tsp (5 mL) coriander seed
1 tsp (5 mL) fennel seed
1 tsp (5 mL) coarse salt
1 tsp (5 mL) vegetable oil
4 ahi tuna loin pieces, 6 oz/170 g each

Grill: hot

1. In a medium mixing bowl, combine shallots, olive oil, lemon juice and zest, 1 tsp/5mL salt and green peppercorns. Add tomatoes and toss to coat. Set aside.
2. In a coffee grinder, combine coriander, fennel and 1 tsp/5 mL salt. Grind until fairly fine.
3. Rub spice blend and vegetable oil into tuna. Sear the tuna on a hot grill until medium rare, about 4 to 5 minutes per side.
4. Meanwhile, in a fry pan over medium-high heat, warm the tomato mixture. To serve, place mixed greens or steamed rice on 4 warmed plates. Top with the tomato sauté and tuna.

DENNIS GREEN

If star-spotting is a measure of fame, Bishop's is unrivalled in Vancouver. Robert De Niro, Robin Williams and Glenn Close are a few (among many) of the silver-screen stars who have cooled their heels in this compact and tasteful room renowned for its fresh seasonal cuisine and impeccable service. Chef Dennis Green, soft-spoken and without a trace of overblown ego, is a big part of this legacy of success. His uncomplicated, intense, elegantly presented food has launched Bishop's onto countless Top Table lists in food and travel magazines such as *Gourmet, Food & Wine* and *Bon Appétit*. Dennis is a passionate supporter of local farmers and their produce. His "fresh is best" philosophy and his seasonally changing menus are quite simply the best our region has to offer.

PAN-SEARED LING COD

with Prune-Plum Sauce

Ling cod is a beautiful fish to work with for grilling, roasting and pan searing. Occasionally the flesh is an opal blue, caused by the fish feeding on a diet of shrimp and crustaceans. These fish are particularly delicious.

Preparation time: 30 minutes
Wine pairing: Pinot Gris, Chardonnay, Riesling

Serves 4

Sauce

- 2 lbs (900 g) Italian prune plums, pitted, with skin on
- 2 cups (500 mL) apple cider
- ½ cup (125 mL) red wine vinegar
- 1 tsp (5 mL) garlic, minced
- 2 tbsp (30 mL) ginger, minced
- 2 tbsp (30 mL) cilantro, chopped
- 2 tbsp (30 mL) tarragon, chopped
- 1 whole clove
- salt and pepper

Ling Cod

- 4 ling cod fillets, skin on, 6 oz/170 g each
- salt and pepper
- 1 tbsp (15 mL) grape seed oil
- edible herbs and flowers for garnish

Oven: 400°F/200°C

1. In a large, heavy, nonreactive saucepan, combine the plums, apple cider, vinegar, garlic, ginger, cilantro, tarragon and clove. Bring to a boil, reduce heat and simmer for 10 minutes or until the plums are broken down and soft. Pulse with a hand blender or purée in a food processor to a smooth sauce consistency.
2. Strain through a fine sieve. Press to extract the plum sauce from the pulp. Season with salt and pepper. Set aside.
3. Season the fish with salt and pepper. To a large ovenproof skillet over medium-high heat, add the grape seed oil and heat until hot. Add cod, skin-side down. Allow the skin to crisp, about 3 to 4 minutes. Turn over and transfer to the oven for 3 to 4 minutes or until fish just begins to flake.
4. To serve, ladle plum sauce on 4 warmed plates, top with a fillet of cod and accompany with seasonal vegetables. Garnish with edible herbs and flowers.

EDWARD TUSON

No stranger to the local culinary scene, Edward trained at several top establishments, including Chateau Whistler, the William Tell and Bacchus at the Wedgewood Hotel. A love of travel has seen Edward don a sarong and trek through the exotic lands of India and Southeast Asia. Along the trail, he has picked up a knowledge and passion for spicing and a palate that has helped him take one of Canada's most internationally renowned resorts to new heights. Edward is one of the longest-serving chefs at the acclaimed Sooke Harbour House and credits his mentor Sinclair Philip for sharpening his skills and instilling in him a real commitment to local ingredients. The pair has cultivated an impressive array of farmers, fishers and foragers who provide the inn with the ingredients to make some of the most impressive food served anywhere.

GRILLED PRAWNS
with Spicy Peach Salsa

Spot prawns are a sweet and tender local delicacy. If you buy head-on prawns, be sure to clean and cook them quickly. Digestive enzymes will cause the flesh to dissolve if left unattended for too long. Tiger prawns are usually farmed shrimp from Southeast Asia and are meatier but tougher than our local prawns.

Preparation time: 20 minutes
Wine pairing: Riesling, Chenin Blanc

Serves 4

Salsa

2 large ripe peaches, pitted and diced
1 small red onion, peeled and diced
1 jalapeño pepper, seeded and diced
1 tbsp (15 mL) olive oil
1 tsp (5 mL) chili oil or hot sauce
1 tbsp (15 mL) basil, chopped
juice and zest of 1 lime
salt and pepper

Prawns

16 large spot or tiger prawns
1 tbsp (15 mL) olive oil
1 tsp (5 mL) sesame oil
1 tsp (5 mL) hot sauce
1 tsp (5 mL) honey
1 tbsp (15 mL) light soy sauce
8 wooden skewers, soaked in water for 30 minutes

Grill: hot

1. In a small bowl, combine peaches, red onion, jalapeño pepper, olive oil, chili oil, basil, lime juice and zest. Season well with salt and pepper and set aside.
2. In a medium bowl, combine prawns, olive oil, sesame oil, hot sauce, honey and soy sauce. Toss well to coat and let marinate for 10 minutes.
3. On a flat work surface, thread a skewer through the tails of four prawns. Thread a second skewer through the body of the prawns. Repeat with remaining prawns to make 4 double skewers.
4. Shake skewers free of excess marinade and place on the hot grill. Cook until the prawns turn pink and just begin to char, 1 to 2 minutes per side. Transfer skewers to 4 warmed plates and serve with rice and grilled vegetables. Top prawns with salsa. Serve remaining salsa on the side.

GRILLED SQUID
with Apple-Mango Vinaigrette

If you are using large squid such as the neon flying squid from the B.C. coast, cut large tubes into 3-inch (7.5 cm) strips, then cut crosswise into thin slices. To prevent them from curling while cooking, thread the slices onto bamboo skewers before grilling. Prawns or large scallops are also wonderful prepared this way.

Preparation time: 30 minutes
Wine pairing: Pinot Blanc, un-oaked Chardonnay, Bacchus

Serves 4

Vinaigrette

¼ cup (60 mL) cider vinegar
1 tbsp (15 mL) sugar (or to taste)
¼ cup (60 mL) extra-virgin olive oil
1 ripe mango, peeled and diced
1 red apple, skin on, cored and diced
2 tbsp (30 mL) green onions, finely chopped
2 tbsp (30 mL) mint, finely chopped

Squid

8 small whole squid tubes, cleaned and skinned
2 tsp (10 mL) tarragon, minced
1 tbsp (15 mL) lemon juice
½ tsp (2.5 mL) lemon zest, freshly grated
1 tbsp (15 mL) toasted sesame oil
salt and pepper
2 cups (500 mL) shredded cabbage or lettuce

Grill: medium-hot

1. In a medium mixing bowl, combine vinegar, sugar and oil; taste and adjust seasonings. Add mango, apple, onions and mint and toss to mix. Refrigerate until ready to use.
2. In a mixing bowl, combine squid, tarragon, lemon juice, zest and oil. Marinate for 10 minutes. Season with salt and pepper just before cooking.
3. Grill squid until well marked and just cooked through, about 1 to 2 minutes on each side. Use a spatula to press down on the tubes to ensure good contact with the grill; be careful not to overcook.
4. To serve, line a serving platter with shredded cabbage. Arrange squid on top and sprinkle generously with vinaigrette.

vegetarian dishes

STEAMED MARKET VEGETABLES WITH SPICY HERB BUTTER

MARKET VEGETABLE ROAST WITH RED PEPPER MAYONNAISE

SAFFRON EGGPLANT TORTELLINI

FRESH CORN BUTTER SAUCE

GARAM MASALA

FRAGRANT SPICED KALE AND POTATOES

EGGPLANT STUFFED WITH RATATOUILLE AND ASIAGO CHEESE

SPAGHETTINI WITH SUN-DRIED TOMATO PESTO AND BOCCONCINI

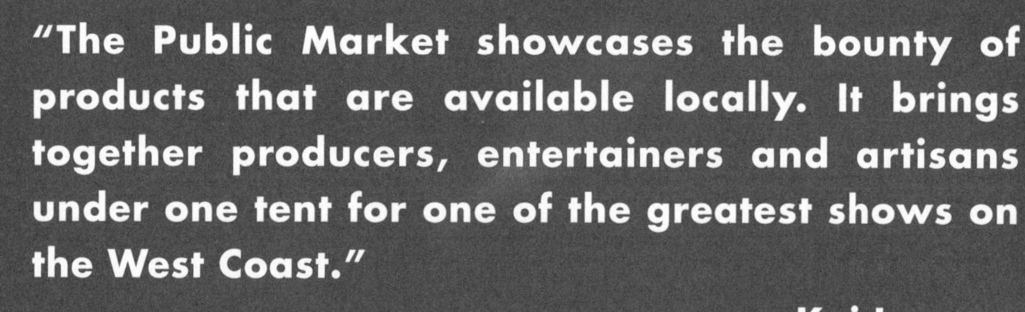

"The Public Market showcases the bounty of products that are available locally. It brings together producers, entertainers and artisans under one tent for one of the greatest shows on the West Coast."

—Kai Lermen

IN PRAISE OF HEIRLOOM VEGETABLES

Walk into any supermarket in North America and you can observe a growing trend in commercial food production. You will find the same tomatoes, cucumbers and peppers (to name a few) for sale in a bland state of conformity. Luckily, this corporate-growing trend has allowed a lot of concerned farmers the opportunity to explore and take advantage of the consumer demand for quality vegetables. A brief survey of seed catalogues will unearth hundreds of varieties of vegetables and food plants. The diversity is astonishing, and many of the plants are heirloom (or heritage) varieties that were grown by our ancestors. Many were shunned by the commercial growers because of their finicky growing nature, their tendency to have fragile skins, or because they contained a few too many seeds. Seek out these wonderful vegetables and you will taste the main component big business has abandoned – flavour. In season, the Market's grocers, day table vendors and farmers' truck market sellers carry an impressive range of produce that should not be missed.

Tomatoes: Although plum, slicing and cherry tomatoes are constant staples on produce shelves these days, late summer remains the season to get truly excited about them. Starting late July and through to October is when specialty growers such as Milan Djordjevich, now locally renowned as "The Tomato Man," bring their carefully nurtured heirloom or heritage tomatoes to the Thursday Farmers' Truck Market. As tribute to this popular fruit cum vegetable, the Public Market has held festivals in its honour and even declared it the Market's favourite fruit. Fair warning: a bite into such exotics as the Old Flame or Golden Nuggets may spoil you forever from finding satisfaction in tomatoes that are imported out of season.

Peppers: All peppers are members of the genus *Capsicum*. Their colours range from cool green to vibrant reds; in between you will find purple, brown and tiger-striped varieties. Hothouse peppers are a growing industry in B.C.; out of season they make acceptable substitutes to thin-walled imported varieties. Hot chilies come in a variety of sizes and heat factors. Jalapeños are relatively mild on the heat scale, particularly compared to the incendiary habanero or Scotch bonnet peppers. When shopping for peppers, choose those that are plump with a smooth skin; avoid blemished or wrinkled skin.

Potatoes: The Pemberton Valley, north of Whistler, has a unique environment that is perfect for the production of quality seed potatoes, possibly because the region resembles the potatoes' home territory of South America, where the spud was first tamed and cultivated. Store potatoes in a cool, dark place to avoid eyes (tiny rootlets) from sprouting. Look for white, red, yellow, pink and purple-skinned potatoes in the Market stalls or at the farmers' truck sales.

Cucumbers: Oddly enough, the cucumber is the one vegetable that has benefited from modern research. Some older varieties contained a chemical called cucurbitacins, a very bitter substance that scientists isolated and bred out of many varieties. Some varieties are bred specifically for pickling (gherkins) or hothouse cultivation (English cucumbers). Unusual varieties include the crystal apple and the lemon cucumber. Both have pretty, round shapes and are crisp and delicious. The lemons have a distinctive acidic flavour.

Others worth looking for: Seek out asparagus, beans, broccoli, cabbages, carrots, cauliflower, corn, eggplants, garlic, leeks, onions, peas, radishes and salsify.

STEAMED MARKET VEGETABLES
with Spicy Herb Butter

Chayote is a Caribbean staple that is actually a fruit. It has a crunchy flavour that is wonderful when steamed. You can, of course, use your favourite vegetables in this simple dish. Garden-fresh carrots, broccoli and cauliflower are all excellent choices. For a fall treat, try steaming wild chanterelles for a truly sensual dining experience.

Preparation time: 20 minutes
Wine pairing: Sauvignon Blanc, Semillon

Serves 6

Herb Butter

2 tbsp (30 mL) butter at room temperature
1 tsp (5 mL) hot sauce
1 tsp (5 mL) garlic, minced
1 tbsp (15 mL) parsley, chopped
1 tbsp (15 mL) sage, chopped
1 tbsp (15 mL) thyme, chopped
1 tbsp (15 mL) lemon juice
salt and pepper

Vegetables

2 cups (500 mL) kohlrabi, peeled and sliced
2 cups (500 mL) chayote, peeled and sliced
2 cups (500 mL) sugar pumpkin, peeled, seeded and cubed
2 cups (500 mL) gai lan, cut in chunks

1. In a small bowl, combine butter, hot sauce, garlic, parsley, sage, thyme, lemon juice, salt and pepper. Refrigerate until needed.
2. In a steamer with stacking racks (or a pot with a tight-fitting lid and a steaming basket), bring 1 cup/250 mL of water to a boil. Place the kohlrabi, chayote and pumpkin in the rack and steam for 5 minutes. Add the gai lan and steam until vegetables are tender, about 5 minutes.
3. Remove from heat and transfer to a serving bowl. Add herb butter, toss well to mix and serve immediately.

MARKET VEGETABLE ROAST

with Red Pepper Mayonnaise

Roasting intensifies the natural flavours and sweetness of the vegetables. Feel free to add to the mix other vegetables, such as zucchini, carrots, onions, eggplant, green beans, mushrooms, Belgian endive or even firm tofu. The vegetables can be dipped into the mayonnaise or the sauce can be drizzled on top.

Preparation time: 45 minutes
Wine pairing: Semillon, Pinot Blanc

Serves 4

12 medium new potatoes, scrubbed and washed
3 cups (750 mL) butternut squash, cubed
1 large red bell pepper, seeded and cut into strips
8 whole garlic cloves, skin on
2 tbsp (30 mL) olive oil
salt and pepper
16 asparagus spears, trimmed and cut in half
½ cup (125 mL) mayonnaise
1 tbsp (15 mL) finely chopped chives

Oven: 400°F/200°C

1. To a large saucepan of boiling, salted water, add potatoes and cook until just tender, about 7 to 10 minutes. Drain potatoes and transfer to a large, shallow roasting pan. Add squash, bell pepper, garlic, oil, salt and pepper. Toss together until vegetables are well coated. Roast about 20 minutes, then remove bell pepper and garlic and set aside to cool. Peel garlic and set aside.
2. Push potatoes and squash to one side and add asparagus. Roll asparagus in pan briefly until coated with oil. Return pan to oven and roast until asparagus is tender, about 7 to 8 minutes.
3. Meanwhile, in a food processor or blender, purée bell pepper, garlic and mayonnaise until smooth; add a little water if mixture is too thick. Pour into a small bowl, fold in the chives and season with salt and pepper. To serve, place roasted vegetables on a serving platter and drizzle with red pepper mayonnaise.

SAFFRON EGGPLANT TORTELLINI

Saffron is made of the hand-harvested stamens of autumn crocuses and is reputed to be the world's most expensive spice. In the Market, Zara's Pasta Nest usually has a supply on hand. Luckily a little saffron goes a long way, and a few threads will provide lots of colour and flavour for this dish. To save time, you can buy premade tortellini of various flavours from several merchants in the Market; dress with the corn sauce for a respectable substitute.

Preparation time: 1 hour
Wine pairing: Full-bodied Riesling, fruity Pinot Blanc, un-oaked Chardonnay

Serves 4 to 6

Pasta

½ tsp (2.5 mL) saffron
2 tbsp (30 mL) boiling water
1 large egg
4 egg yolks
1 tbsp (15 mL) extra-virgin olive oil
¼ tsp (1 mL) white wine vinegar
2¼ cups (560 mL) all-purpose flour
1 tsp (5 mL) salt

Filling

2 tbsp (30 mL) extra-virgin olive oil
1 medium onion, finely chopped
1 small eggplant, peeled and finely diced
1 tsp (5 mL) garlic, minced
¼ cup (60 mL) fresh herbs, chopped (thyme, marjoram, rosemary, sage, etc.)
3 tbsp (45 mL) mascarpone cheese
salt and pepper
1 egg, beaten (for egg wash)

1. In a small bowl, combine saffron and boiling water. Steep to allow the colour to infuse, then cool to room temperature. In a small bowl, combine the saffron liquid, egg, egg yolks, oil and vinegar.
2. In a large bowl, combine the flour and salt. Pour in the egg mixture and knead until a soft dough is formed; the result should be a smooth and soft ball. Add more flour if the dough is sticky. Cover and set aside to rest for at least 15 minutes.
3. In a large fry pan over medium-high heat, sauté the oil, onion and eggplant for 5 minutes. Reduce heat to low; add garlic and sauté for 10 minutes more or until eggplant is soft and well browned. Mix in herbs and set aside to cool. Fold in the mascarpone cheese and season with salt and pepper.
4. Roll out the pasta with a pasta machine (or well-floured heavy rolling pin) into a very thin sheet and cut into 3 in/8 cm squares or rounds. Brush egg wash around edges of one square and spoon about 1 tsp/5 mL of filling into the centre. Brush edges with the beaten egg; fold to form a triangle and pinch to seal. Take 2 corners of the triangle and press together with a small amount of egg wash to form a crescent. Set aside on a baking sheet lined with wax paper and continue with the rest of the tortellini. Refrigerate until ready to use.
5. To a large pot filled with boiling salted water, add the tortellini and cook for 4 to 5 minutes or until the tortellini float to the surface. Drain, return to empty pot and gently toss with corn sauce (see following recipe) or accompany with a simple dressing of olive oil and Parmesan cheese. Transfer to 4 bowls and serve immediately.

FRESH CORN BUTTER SAUCE

This rich butter sauce is a wonderful companion to pasta, polenta, steamed vegetables or grilled fish. The sauce can be made 30 minutes in advance and held off the heat until needed. A common chef's trick is to reserve the sauce in a thermal flask to keep it warm and to prevent the contents from separating. The cooking liquid can be used as a fine stock or as a base for vegetarian soup.

Preparation time: 20 minutes

Serves 4

2 corn cobs, peeled and washed
1 medium onion, diced
2 sprigs fresh thyme
½ cup (125 mL) dry white wine
½ cup (125 g) unsalted butter,
diced and at room temperature
salt and pepper

1. To a medium saucepan filled with salted boiling water, add the corn, onion, thyme and wine. Return to a boil, reduce heat and simmer for 10 minutes or until corn is tender. Remove corn, reserve liquid and allow to cool. Cut the kernels from the cobs and set aside.

2. Purée corn in a blender or food processor with 2 tbsp/30 mL of the cooking liquid. Strain through a fine sieve into a small saucepan. Reheat sauce over medium heat until hot; remove from heat. Whisk in the soft butter until blended. Season with salt and pepper and keep warm until needed.

DOUGLAS ANDERSON

Born in Aberdeen, Scotland, and raised in northern Illinois, Douglas Anderson signed on with the U.S. Coast Guard fresh out of high school, and the choice of becoming a maintenance engineer, a deckhand or a cook led him to the obvious. With a background as colourful as his stories of the American heartland, Douglas landed on the Vancouver food scene in April 1998. An accomplished tenure as chef at Chicago's Four Seasons Hotel was highlighted by Seasons, the hotel's premier dining room, being touted as number one in North America while under Douglas's care. Since his arrival with an open heart, an infectious passion and an insatiable curiosity, Douglas has been knocking on local farmers' doors to discover first-hand the bounty of our region. His seasonal menus in the Four Seasons' flagship restaurant, Chartwell, are showcases of his unique North American style and artful handling of local ingredients. The Producer Dinners he pioneered featuring area suppliers have become Vancouver culinary classics.

GARAM MASALA

Almost every style of regional cooking in India has its own version of garam masala, but it is often called by other names. Some versions tend to be a bit sweeter; others are pungent, hot or fragrantly spiced. "Garam" means warm and "masala" means spices. Garam masala can be added to almost any north Indian curry in small amounts. Add it to roasted or pan-fried vegetables for a wonderful aromatic effect. On Granville Island, The Grainry and South China Seas have many of the ingredients. While roasting the whole spices, the aroma will be quite strong and will quickly spread throughout your home.

Preparation time: 15 minutes

Makes ½ cup/125 mL

1 tsp (5 mL) cloves (heaping spoonful)
1½ tsp (7.5 mL) cardamom seeds
(from about 10 whole black cardamom pods)
6 tbsp (90 mL) cumin seeds (heaping spoonfuls)
1 tbsp (15 mL) cinnamon sticks, chopped or finely broken
¼ tsp (1 mL) ground mace
¼ tsp (1 mL) ground nutmeg

1. In a heavy iron skillet over medium-high heat, toast the cloves, cardamom seeds, cumin, cinnamon, mace and nutmeg, stirring constantly. When the cumin seeds darken slightly, remove from heat and transfer to a plate.
2. When mixture is cool, grind in an electric spice mill or coffee grinder, or use the traditional mortar and pestle. Store in an airtight jar in a cool dark place. Use within a couple of months.

FRAGRANT SPICED KALE AND POTATOES

This is a family meal that is great with traditional Indian flatbread such as chapati or naan. It is a warming dish that helps to fight the chill of winter and keep your body strong.

Preparation time: 30 minutes
Wine pairing: Dry Riesling, Gamay

Serves 4 to 6

¼ cup (60 mL) canola oil
1 tsp (5 mL) cumin seeds
1 cup (250 mL) stewed tomatoes (homemade or canned), crushed
½ tsp (2.5 mL) ground turmeric
1 tsp (5 mL) ground cumin
1 tsp (5 mL) ground coriander
1 tbsp (15 mL) garam masala (see previous recipe)
1 tsp (5 mL) sea salt
1 medium potato, washed and cubed
1 cup (250 mL) water
1 lb (450 g) fresh kale leaves, washed and chopped

1. To a large, heavy-bottomed saucepan over medium-high heat, add oil and heat for 1 minute or until just smoking. Add the cumin seeds and let sizzle for 30 seconds. Immediately stir in tomatoes, turmeric, cumin, coriander, garam masala and salt. Reduce heat to medium-low and simmer, stirring frequently, for 10 minutes (the oil should separate from the spices).
2. Add potato and water. Stir well, cover and cook for 3 to 4 minutes. Add kale and stir well to mix. Add additional water if the mixture starts to stick to the bottom of the saucepan. Cover and cook for an additional 15 minutes or until kale is tender. Stir and test the kale every 5 minutes during cooking.
3. Transfer to a serving dish and eat with warm chapati or naan.

VIKRAM VIJ

Vikram has taken the Vancouver culinary scene by storm in the few years since he opened Vij's Restaurant. He has filled a void in the local scene by providing top-quality Indian cuisine prepared with the bounty of the region. The result is a seasonally changing menu that is alive with spice and vitality and a happy partner to fine B.C. wines and microbrews. Vikram learned his craft under the watchful eye of John Bishop and acquired his international experience in Europe. In spring 1999, the restaurant took its place on the world stage when Vikram was invited to showcase his food at a special dinner at the famed James Beard House in New York. Vikram is a frequent customer at the Market and consistently orders ingredients, both exotic and commonplace, from Market merchants.

EGGPLANT STUFFED WITH RATATOUILLE AND ASIAGO CHEESE

These stuffed eggplants make an excellent side dish for a party. They can be made ahead and baked with cheese just before serving. Ratatouille is a traditional sautéed vegetable dish of the Mediterranean that utilizes the bounty of seasonal vegetables and fine local olive oil. Try topping the eggplant with mozzarella (or fresh bocconcini), goat cheese, white Cheddar or Brie.

Preparation time: 35 minutes
Wine pairing: Pinot Noir, Pinot Meunier

Serves 4

2 medium eggplants, cut in half
4 tbsp (60 mL) olive oil
salt and pepper
1 large white onion, diced
1 tbsp (15 mL) garlic, minced (or more to taste)
2 red bell peppers, seeded and diced
1 Japanese eggplant, diced
1 green zucchini, diced
1 yellow zucchini, diced
1 large ripe tomato, diced
1 tbsp (15 mL) fresh thyme, chopped
1 tbsp (15 mL) fresh rosemary, chopped
1 cup (250 mL) Asiago cheese, grated

Oven: 400°F/200°C

1. On a baking sheet lined with parchment paper, place eggplant halves, skin-side up. Drizzle with 2 tbsp/30 mL olive oil and season well with salt and pepper. Bake for 15 to 20 minutes or until soft to touch. Remove from oven; cool. Turn over and gently press in centre of each piece of eggplant to make a cavity for the stuffing. Season cavity with salt and pepper and set aside.
2. In a large nonstick fry pan, heat remaining olive oil over medium heat. Sauté onion, garlic and peppers briefly, until fragrant. Mix in Japanese eggplant, zucchini, tomato, thyme and rosemary. Season with salt and pepper and continue to cook until vegetables are tender, about 5 minutes. Remove from heat.
3. Divide and spoon ratatouille (vegetable) mixture into each eggplant half. Top each stuffed eggplant with ¼ cup/60 mL of cheese and place in preheated oven for 10 minutes or until the cheese is melted and forms a golden brown crust. Remove from oven and serve.

DINO RENAERTS

Dino has been active on the local food scene for many years and has won numerous awards on local cooking competitions during his apprenticeship phase. As an energetic sous-chef at the Waterfront Centre Hotel, Dino blossomed under the guidance of Daryle Nagata and was soon hand-picked to fill the vacancy of chef at Hotel Vancouver's elegant 900 West. Upon his arrival, Dino quickly put his mark on the restaurant with his innovative style, which deftly combines European and Asian techniques. Finally in command of his elements and ever brimming with the thirst for knowledge, he recently completed his certification as a sommelier and is the first in Vancouver to achieve the unique stature of chef/sommelier.

CO-OWNER ZARA'S PASTA NEST

SPAGHETTINI WITH SUN-DRIED TOMATO PESTO AND BOCCONCINI

Bocconcini is fresh mozzarella cheese rolled into small balls. Originally made from water buffalo milk, the cheese has a soft; creamy quality that binds pasta together. Fresh pasta cooks very quickly. For dry pasta, double the cooking time. *Al dente* literally means "to the tooth"; pasta should be cooked just enough to retain a chewy, not mushy, texture. Zara's carries a full line of Italian products including pasta, pesto and authentic cheeses.

Preparation time: 15 minutes
Wine pairing: Sauvignon Blanc, Chardonnay

Serves 4

1 lb (450 g) fresh spaghettini or any strand pasta
2 tbsp (30 mL) extra-virgin olive oil
½ cup (125 mL) sun-dried tomato pesto (available at Zara's)
salt and pepper
½ cup (125 mL) chopped bocconcini or mozzarella
2 tbsp (30 mL) Parmigiano-Reggiano cheese, freshly grated

1. In a large pot filled with boiling, salted water, cook the pasta, stirring well, until *al dente*, about 4 to 5 minutes. (A little drizzle of oil in the water will help reduce the foaming of starch as the pasta cooks.) Drain and toss with a little olive oil to help separate the strands.

2. Return the cleaned pot to the stove over medium-high heat. Add the pesto and warm through. Add the pasta and toss well to coat. Season with salt and pepper; add the bocconcini and drizzle with olive oil. Toss to mix well and serve just as the cheese starts to melt into the sauce. Top with the grated cheese and a few extra grindings of fresh pepper. Serve with a slice of rustic Italian bread.

LORIS ZARA

The Zara family – John, Luisa and son Loris – has been a fixture at the Market for many years. Their store is a great place to obtain a wide range of Italian products, including pesto, real prosciutto and handmade pasta. Their creative and wholesome products are freshly made to ensure the highest standards of quality. The family is also known for the great personal service they provide to patrons of the Market. If you need ideas for winning combinations of pasta and sauces, just ask for Loris.

side orders

TOMATO-OLIVE CONFIT

ZUCCHINI AND BLACK OLIVE SPAGHETTI

POTATO SALAD WITH DILL AND QUARK DRESSING

MUSHROOM MASHED POTATOES

CREAMED KOHLRABI

TOMATO AND SMOKED CHEDDAR SCONES

SPICED CORNBREAD

Marinades
Vinaigrettes
NEW!
Gourmet butters
frozen fish sauces
coconut sauce
Crème fraîche
SOUPS
Mayos
Fresh tomato pasta sauces

"I cannot overestimate the importance of Granville Island Public Market. It has been an integral part of the overall improvement and appreciation for good food here in Vancouver."

—Margaret Chisholm

GOOD COOKING IS IN THE DETAILS

All great chefs have secret ingredients that provide the foundation to their cooking. Here we take a brief look at some Market ingredients that are fundamental to the way we cook. These are good, simple ingredients that are worth seeking out to enhance the basic way you cook and eat.

Sea salt: Salt is something we often take for granted. While it has a bad rap for contributing to high blood pressure and stress-related ailments, it is also a necessary component of our diet. In recent years, chefs have discovered the virtues of unprocessed sea salt. When compared head-to-head with processed table salt, the sea salt exhibits a deep range of flavours. Regular salt comes off as overly salty and metallic. Try some for yourself on a freshly cut ripe tomato.

Dried spices: All dried spices will benefit from a simple dry-toasting in a fry pan before being ground for seasoning duties or curries. Try toasting whole peppercorns before cooling them and adding them to your pepper mill. The heat activates essential oils in the spices and brings out the true essence of flavour.

Olive oil: A foundation of the Mediterranean diet and possessing great nutritional value, olive oil is the best all-round oil for cooking, dressing and flavouring foods. Cold-pressed olive oil is the finest quality, best for salads and flavouring, with a fruity and vibrant taste. Use pure olive oil for cooking, and choose a good quality oil from Italy, Portugal, Greece, Spain, France or California.

Vinegar: Vinegar can be a versatile tool in your kitchen as well as a handy cooking ingredient. Pure white vinegar is great for disinfecting and refreshing your wooden cutting boards after cleaning. Apple cider vinegar is pungent and flavourful, great for salad dressings and as an aid to digestion. Rice vinegar is mild and pleasant tasting, great for subtle salad dressing and for making the perfect sushi rice. Wine vinegar is flavourful and aromatic. Add unused wine to an active wine vinegar to make your own special house blend. Balsamic vinegar can be a rare and expensive treat. The authentic version is aged for many years in a variety of wooden casks and can fetch exorbitant prices. Use cheaper balsamic for cooking, but splurge on a high-quality vinegar for dressing vegetables, salads and good bread.

Garlic: The aromatic bulbs are more than an essential aromatic for cooking; they are widely regarded as possessing healing properties. Garlic is believed to promote circulation, eliminate toxins from the body and have the ability to inhibit the common cold virus and other microorganisms associated with degenerative diseases such as cancer. Other claims include lowering blood pressure and cholesterol, increasing respiratory capacity, inhibiting allergies and increasing mental activity. Store garlic in a cool dark place and remove any green shoots from the centre of older bulbs. These shoots may contain bitter elements.

Ginger: Fresh ginger is another heralded "super food" that is much more than a great flavouring agent. Ginger is revered by the Chinese as a restorer of energy, and it has powerful antibacterial properties. Choose large pieces of ginger that are plump, smooth-skinned and blemish free. Young ginger, thin-skinned and tipped with pink, is mild and ideal for pickling and for spicing delicate sauces and stir-fries. Excess ginger can be stored in the refrigerator for up to two weeks.

TOMATO-OLIVE CONFIT

This tomato confit is excellent tossed with hot pasta or simply spooned onto a slice of French bread. Place leftovers in a sealed glass container and keep in the refrigerator for up to 1 week. Mincing the garlic allows the flavour to permeate the tomatoes. Alternatively, you can use 1 or 2 whole, peeled cloves for a mild, nutty effect.

Preparation time: 3 hours

Makes 4 cups/1 L

1 tbsp (15 mL) garlic, minced
2 lbs (900 g) fresh heritage tomatoes, halved
(or 1 28 oz/796 mL can of stewed tomatoes)
½ cup (125 mL) extra-virgin olive oil
2 tbsp (30 mL) black olives, chopped
1 tbsp (15 mL) capers
1 tsp (5 mL) thyme, finely chopped
salt and pepper

OLIVES

Green olives come in many shapes and flavours. Often they are marinated in herbs, garlic and chilies. A particularly delicious version pairs garlic and orange zest. Black olives are brine-cured ripe olives that are often flavoured with olive oil and seasonings. Kalamata olives are a Greek specialty that are usually preserved whole with the pit included. Use an olive or cherry pitter to remove the stone without damaging the flesh.

Oven: 250°F/120°C

1. In an ovenproof casserole dish, scatter the garlic across the bottom. Layer the tomatoes cut-side down and cover with olive oil. Season well with salt and pepper and bake until the tomatoes are soft and dense, about 3 hours.
2. Remove from oven and stir in the olives, capers and thyme. Adjust seasonings with salt and pepper if necessary. Allow confit to cool to room temperature and store in a sealed glass container in the refrigerator.

MARGARET CHISHOLM

Montreal-born, Margaret enjoys a rich culinary legacy handed down through generations of women in her family. Her namesake, Margaret Chisholm Sr., owned and operated Peggy's Lunch, a small canteen in Nova Scotia. A graduate of Peter Trump's New York Cooking School, Margaret has been a chef, cooking teacher and food writer for more than a dozen years. At Culinary Capers she oversees an operation that caters everything from picnics for two to dinner for thousands. Margaret's kitchen is a stone's throw away from the Market and she loves to run in for last-minute ingredients. If she can steal away, she grabs a quick bite and a brief paddle in the kayak she keeps at a nearby dock to recharge the batteries that keep her ticking through her long and demanding days

ZUCCHINI AND BLACK OLIVE "SPAGHETTI"

These thin strands of vegetables cook very quickly and resemble pasta in appearance. Use yellow and green zucchini for a colourful side dish. Strips of roasted red or yellow peppers are another tasty addition.

Preparation time: 15 minutes

Makes 3 cups/750 mL

3 medium zucchini
3 tbsp (45 mL) extra-virgin olive oil
2 garlic cloves, chopped
½ cup (125 mL) kalamata olives, pitted and chopped
sea salt and pepper

1. Cut zucchini with a vegetable slicer or mandoline (with serrated shredding blade) to form long spaghettilike strands. Alternatively, you can cut the zucchini lengthwise into thin slices using a vegetable peeler, then cut each slice into long strips.
2. In large fry pan over medium-high heat, sauté olive oil, garlic and olives until fragrant and sizzling. Stir in zucchini "spaghetti" and sauté until tender but still a little crunchy, about 2 minutes. Season with salt and pepper. Remove from heat and keep warm until needed.

morie ford and bill mcintosh

OWNERS, THE MILKMAN

POTATO SALAD

with Dill and Quark Dressing

Quark is a low-fat milk by-product that is high in protein, similar to ricotta or cottage cheese. It is traditionally used in Europe to add richness to cakes and baked goods. Here quark is used along with yogourt to make a creamy blanket for new potatoes.

Preparation time: 30 minutes

Serves 4

Dressing

- 1 cup (250 mL) mayonnaise
- ¼ cup (60 mL) plain quark or dry cottage cheese
- ¼ cup (60 mL) yogourt
- 1 tsp (5 mL) dry mustard
- juice of 1 lemon
- 2 tbsp (30 mL) fresh dill, chopped, or 1 tbsp/15 mL dried
- salt and pepper

Salad

- 1 lb (450 g) small new potatoes, cooked
- 2 hard-boiled eggs, chopped
- 4 shallots or green onions, finely chopped
- 1 cup (250 mL) celery, diced
- 1 tsp (5 mL) paprika
- salt and pepper

1. In a large mixing bowl, whisk the mayonnaise, quark, yogourt, mustard, lemon juice, dill, salt and pepper until smooth.
2. Leave small new potatoes whole; cut larger potatoes into bite-size chunks. Add to the bowl along with the chopped eggs, shallots and celery. Season with paprika, salt and pepper. Toss well and serve at room temperature. This dish can be made well in advance and stored in a sealed container in the refrigerator.

MORIE FORD AND BILL MCINTOSH

Morie Ford and Bill McIntosh have been actively involved in the operation of The Milkman for the past 10 years. The pair took over the shop from Bill's father, who was among the first to join the family of merchants at the Market when it opened in 1979. Like so many others, the pair escaped the frozen Prairies, leaving behind former careers in Alberta, where Bill practised law and Morie was a schoolteacher. Today they are hard at work sourcing and bringing to market the best specialty dairy products they can find from all over Canada.

MUSHROOM MASHED POTATOES

Use good baking potatoes for a fluffy mash or waxy, white or yellow new potatoes for a creamy mash. If the potatoes are going to sit for any length of time, make the initial mash fairly wet, as the dish will dry out in 20 to 30 minutes. Alternatively, you can add a little hot liquid just before serving to soften and fluff the potatoes. Add raw pine mushrooms or truffles to the finished mash for a sublime effect.

Preparation time: 20 minutes

Serves 4 to 6

2 lbs (900 g) potatoes, peeled and chopped
1 tbsp (15 mL) olive oil
2 cups (500 mL) mushrooms (button, chanterelle, morel, etc.), sliced
½ cup (125 mL) warm milk
2 tbsp (30 mL) butter
salt and pepper

1. Place the potatoes in a stockpot filled with cold, salted water and bring to a boil over high heat. Cook until the potatoes are soft, about 8 to 10 minutes. Strain potatoes into a coarse sieve and set aside to drain.
2. In a fry pan over medium-high heat, cook the olive oil and mushrooms for 2 minutes, stirring occasionally.
3. Meanwhile, crush potatoes with a food ricer or potato masher. Stir in milk and butter over medium-low heat until butter is melted. Fold in the mushrooms and season with salt and pepper. Serve warm.

CREAMED KOHLRABI

This unusual vegetable is bathed in cream and nutmeg to make a rich and unique-tasting dish. Kohlrabi is a common vegetable in Europe and is gaining acceptance with North American cooks for its crisp, refreshing qualities.

Preparation time: 20 minutes

Serves 4

2 cups (500 mL) kohlrabi, peeled
and cut into julienne strips
1 cup (250 mL) whipping cream
1 tsp (5 mL) cornstarch mixed with 1 tsp (5 mL) water
pinch nutmeg
salt and pepper

1. In a medium pot of boiling, salted water, blanch kohlrabi until tender, about 3 to 4 minutes. Drain and place in a bowl filled with water and ice cubes. When cool, drain and reserve.
2. In a medium saucepan, bring cream to a boil over high heat, being careful not to let it boil over. Immediately reduce heat and simmer until the volume is reduced by half.
3. Whisk in the cornstarch mixture until cream thickens. Season with nutmeg, salt and pepper to taste. Add the kohlrabi and stir until warmed through. Serve immediately.

KAI LERMEN

For many years, the highly acclaimed Fleuri Restaurant in the Sutton Place Hotel took its lead from the talented Kai Lermen. A protégé of French master chef Marc Haeberlin of the famed Auberge de l'Ill in Alsace, Kai began his strict training at the tender age of 16. Since arriving in Vancouver, Kai's thoughtful use of local bounty in his innovative menus has won him rave reviews from gourmets worldwide. Kai loved to shop at the Market with out-of-town visitors. He claimed this inspires his guests to play a role in the kitchen when he entertains. Since Kai visited with us he has been lured away to greener pastures. We thank him and wish him all the best.

TOMATO AND SMOKED CHEDDAR SCONES

Andrew likes to make these savoury scones with a tomato that he has diced and poached in olive oil. Fresh tomatoes make an acceptable alternative, or you can use sun-dried tomatoes that have been packed in oil.

Preparation time: 30 minutes

Serves 4

1 large tomato, seeded and finely diced
5 cups (1.25 L) all-purpose flour
3 tbsp (45 mL) baking powder
1 tsp (5 mL) salt
½ tsp (2.5 mL) pepper, freshly ground
⅔ cup (165 mL) soft butter
5 large eggs
1 cup (250 mL) whipping cream
½ cup (125 mL) smoked Cheddar cheese, grated
1 egg mixed with 2 tbsp (25 mL) water
coarse sea salt

BAKING TIPS

Keep the kitchen cool while working with pastry and dough. A kitchen fan and a cool surface to work on (marble is best) will produce a superior product. When rolling, use a heavy pin, applying firm, even pressure. Make sure all surfaces are covered with a good dusting of flour. Brush off excess dough before proceeding with recipe. If the dough is sticking to the pin or tearing, fold it up and refrigerate it for at least 15 minutes before proceeding.

Oven: 350°F/180°C

1. Place the tomato in a strainer set over a bowl. Let drain.
2. In a large mixing bowl, sift together flour, baking powder, salt and pepper. Add the butter and cut into pea-size chunks with a pastry cutter or two knives. In a small bowl, whisk together the eggs and cream and gradually add to the flour mixture.
3. Stir in the cheese and tomato and stir until the dough just sticks together. Turn out onto a floured work surface and gently knead the dough into a ball. Roll out with a well-floured rolling pin into an even thickness (about 1 in/2.5 cm). Cut out into scone shapes (rounds, wedges, triangles or squares) and transfer to a baking sheet.
4. Brush scones with egg wash, sprinkle with coarse sea salt and bake until golden brown, about 10 minutes.

ANDREW SPRINGETT

Andrew is the talented chef who presides over the stoves at Diva in Vancouver's Metropolitan Hotel, a restaurant that is regarded by many as among the best in Canada. His cool and easygoing manner is an inspiration to his co-workers and has helped to build a cohesive team in the kitchen. Andrew's mentor, executive chef Michael Noble, has instilled in Andrew a love of fine cooking and a passion for local food and wine. As a team, Noble and Springett have sought out the best local suppliers and weave their products into a menu that is the essence of modern West Coast cuisine. Their attention to detail keeps the restaurant an acclaimed international destination and the winner of countless awards for food, service and wine.

SPICED CORNBREAD

Sean adds spices to create a full and hearty cornbread. Feel free to add more chili (or hot sauce) to make the dish spicier. Chopped fresh cilantro is a nice addition, or try a topping of chopped fresh tomatoes and mozzarella for a tasty fusion of cornbread and pizza.

Preparation time: 40 to 50 minutes

Serves 4 to 6

4 cups (1 L) all-purpose flour
2 tbsp (30 mL) baking powder
⅓ cup (80 mL) sugar
1½ cups (375 mL) cornmeal
1 tsp (5 mL) fennel seeds
1 tsp (5 mL) chili powder
½ tsp (2.5 mL) chili flakes
salt and pepper
2 cups (500 mL) milk
⅓ cup (80 mL) vegetable oil
⅓ cup (80 mL) butter, melted

Oven: 350°F/180°C

1. In a large bowl, sift the flour and baking powder together. Stir in the sugar, cornmeal, fennel seeds, chili powder, chili flakes, salt and pepper. Make a well in the centre and add the milk and oil. Slowly mix to make a smooth batter.
2. Fold in the melted butter. Pour batter into an oiled cast-iron skillet that has been dusted with cornmeal. Bake for 30 to 40 minutes, or until a toothpick comes out clean and the top is well browned.

desserts

WARM GINGER-CHOCOLATE VOLCANO CAKES

HONEY AND STAR ANISE POACHED APPLES

RUSTIC APRICOT AND GINGER TART

PEACH AND BLUEBERRY COBBLER

RHUBARB FOOL

LEMON VERBENA PANNA COTTA
WITH POACHED CHERRIES

BAILEY'S MOCHA CUSTARD

SUGAR SPICE COOKIES

"The market is the perfect resource for anyone interested in good food. The merchants, farmers and craftspeople have never disappointed me in my search for great products."
—Bill Jones

FRUIT: OUR JUST DESSERTS

We are blessed with a cornucopia of great fruits here in the Pacific Northwest. The hot Interior valleys (like the beautiful Okanagan) are ideal for the production of tree fruit and grapes. The cool misted coasts are heaven for many types of berries. On a hot summer day in the Market, these fruits collide in a symphony of colours and summertime flavours. The biggest challenge is buying enough fruit to survive the trip home. Often the bounty of our farms makes it only as far as a sunny bench at the back of the Market.

Berries: The arrival of berries signals that the main harvest season is starting to hit its full stride. Local strawberries still taste like the berries of our childhood; blueberries are large and sweet and taste of distilled sunshine. Blackberries are delicate, impossibly juicy and capable of smearing the shirtfront of the most careful eater. Many hybrid varieties are grown locally. The fertile Fraser Delta produces bumper crops of blueberries, blackberries, raspberries, cranberries, loganberries and currants. Choose whole, unbroken berries, checking for signs of surface mould on the underlying berries. Use within one or two days.

Peaches: Nothing beats the satisfaction of a sun-ripened peach filled with sweet juice. The Okanagan boasts a wide variety of freestone and clingstone peaches that are among the best available anywhere. Peaches can be successfully preserved by freezing slices on a baking sheet lined with parchment paper. Freeze until the peaches are solid and transfer to a plastic storage bag, labelled with the contents and date. The peaches will keep well for two to three months.

Plums: Many varieties of plums are grown in B.C. and sold at the Market from May to October. Blue, purple, green, yellow and red – they come in a rainbow of colours and are great eaten as a snack, baked into tarts, added to salads and made into sauces and salsas. Ripe plums should be firm yet give slightly when gently squeezed.

Cherries: At the peak of summer, Market tables groan under the weight of huge pyramids of cherries. Our region prides itself on growing the sweetest and largest cherries available. Bing cherries are deep ruby red and sweet. Van cherries are small, pitted, sweet and juicy. Rainier cherries are golden with an attractive red blush and are the sweetest and juiciest cherries available. Cherries should be eaten fresh within one to two days, which never seems to be a problem!

Apples: Apples are truly the area where the Market excels. You are guaranteed to find at least a dozen types of apples for sale at any given time of the year. In the fall, at the peak of the season, you will find growers dedicated to the task of preserving and growing an astounding variety of apples. In addition to all the usual commercial apples are heritage apples like Belle de Boskop, Cox Orange Pippen, Chizel Jersey, Dabinett, Golden Russet, Kidd's Orange-Red, Mutsu, Purple Spartan, Wagner and Winston apples, among many others. Choose crisp, firm apples, free of bruises. Store apples in a cool dark place for best results.

Pears: Anjou, Bartlett, Bosc, Asian and Japanese crystal pears are chief among the main B.C. varieties of this favourite fruit. Surprisingly delicate, pears are often picked while unripe for transport. They will ripen nicely when stored uncovered or in a paper bag at room temperature. For cooking, choose fruits that are underripe and free of blemishes. Like apples, pears will turn brown from oxidation when cut or peeled. Dipping them in lightly acidulated water will help prevent discolouration.

WARM GINGER-CHOCOLATE VOLCANO CAKES

Spicy ginger adds a pleasing bite to this rich chocolate dessert. Prepare the filling in advance and place the cakes in the oven just before serving the main course. Serve warm from the oven for the full volcano effect.

Preparation time: 40 minutes
Wine pairing: Vidal icewine

Serves 6

Cakes

- 8 oz (225 g) semi-sweet chocolate (Callebaut or Valhrona)
- ¾ cup (185 mL) unsalted butter
- ¾ cup (185 mL) cake flour
- ½ tsp (2.5 mL) ground ginger
- 5 large eggs
- 3 large egg yolks
- ¼ cup (60 mL) granulated sugar
- 2 tbsp (30 mL) cold coffee, strongly brewed
- ½ cup (125 mL) candied ginger, minced
- 6 ramekin moulds or custard cups
- 6 chocolate chunks (1 in/2.5 cm)

Sauce

- ¾ cup (185 mL) whipping cream
- 6 oz (170 g) dark chocolate
- ¼ cup (60 g) unsalted butter
- 1 tbsp (15 mL) dark rum
- vanilla ice cream

Oven: 375°F/190°C

1. In a double boiler or mixing bowl placed over a pot of simmering water, melt the 8 oz/225 g of chocolate and the butter. Be very careful to avoid scorching. Don't allow any moisture to splash into the bowl. Set aside.
2. In a small bowl, sift together cake flour and ground ginger. Set aside. In a large bowl, whisk together the eggs, yolks and sugar until fluffy and light lemon-coloured. Fold in the melted chocolate and butter, and the coffee. Fold in the flour in batches until evenly coloured. Gently fold in the candied ginger.
3. Prepare small (½ cup/125 mL) ramekin moulds or custard cups by coating with butter and dusting with sugar. Pour the batter into the molds, filling to within ¼ in/5 mm of the tops. Press a chunk of chocolate into each ramekin. Cake can be made in advance up to this point and refrigerated for up to 48 hours.
4. In a medium saucepan over medium-high heat, bring whipping cream to the boil. Immediately pour over the dark chocolate and stir to melt. Add the butter and rum and stir well to mix. Reserve in a warm place until needed, or gently reheat before serving.
5. To serve, place ramekins on a baking sheet and bake for 15 minutes or until set around the edges. Unmould and serve warm with vanilla ice cream and warm sauce.

NATHAN FONG

Born and raised in Vancouver, Nathan graduated from the Dubrulle International Culinary Institute in 1990. After furthering his studies with Anne Willan (of the famed La Varenne Cooking School in France), Nathan went on to form a successful catering company. Combining his keen interest in food and his applied design background, he focused on establishing himself as one of Canada's premier food and props stylists for print, television and film. His long list of satisfied clients includes cookbook author James McNair, McDonald's, Kraft, Air Canada and the B.C. Wine Institute. In 1995 Nathan opened his second office in Los Angeles, and in 1998 he was honoured with the much-coveted IACP (International Association of Culinary Professionals) Award of Excellence in Foodstyling.

HONEY AND STAR ANISE POACHED APPLES

Choose a firm apple like Fuji or Jonagold for the best results. Soft apples break down into apple purée and are unsuitable for poaching. Serve the fruit cool or warm with vanilla ice cream, yogourt or crème fraîche (homemade sour cream).

Preparation time: 30 minutes
Wine pairing: Late-harvest Optima or Riesling

Serves 4 to 6

1 cup (250 mL) non-alcoholic sweet apple cider or apple juice
1 cup (250 mL) fragrant honey
juice and zest of 1 lemon
4 slices fresh ginger
1 whole star anise
pinch of salt
6 large apples, peeled, cored, cut in wedges
vanilla ice cream

1. In a large saucepan, combine the apple cider, honey, lemon juice and zest, ginger, star anise and salt. Bring to a boil over high heat and reduce to a simmer. Add the apples and simmer for 10 to 15 minutes or until apples are just tender but not mushy. You don't want the apples to fall apart.
2. Remove from heat and cool in the poaching liquid. Transfer to a glass or plastic container. Will keep 1 week in refrigerator. Serve cold or reheat over gentle heat; top with vanilla ice cream.

RUSTIC APRICOT AND GINGER TART

This interesting dessert is very easy to make and works with a host of other soft fruit. It is a very comforting dish that will warm up a cool autumn night. Out of season this dish can be made with canned apricots or peaches. Pour the fruit and juice onto the crust and bake.

Preparation time: 60 minutes
Wine pairing: Late-harvest Ehrenfelser or Optima

Serves 6 to 8

- 2 lbs (900 g) apricots, pitted
- ½ cup (125 mL) brown sugar
- 1 tbsp (15 mL) fresh ginger, grated
- 1 tsp (5 mL) lemon zest, grated
- 1 cup (250 mL) flour
- 5 tbsp (75 mL) unsalted butter
- 1 tbsp (15 mL) cream cheese
- ½ cup (125 mL) heavy cream
- 1 large egg, beaten

Oven: 325°F/160°C

1. Wash apricots and slice into quarters, removing pits. In a mixing bowl, combine apricots, sugar, ginger and lemon zest. Set aside.
2. To a medium bowl, add the flour, 4 tbsp/60 mL of the butter and the cream cheese. Cut in butter and cream cheese with a pastry cutter or two knives until the texture resembles coarse meal.
3. In a small bowl, combine the cream and egg. Sprinkle the egg mixture over the flour. Blend with your fingers to form a soft dough.
4. Press the dough with your fingers into a 9x12 in/22x30 cm buttered cake dish. Cover the pastry with the fruit mixture (if you feel the mixture is not juicy enough, add ¼ cup/60 mL hot water); dot with the remaining butter.
5. Bake for 45 minutes, or until the mixture is bubbling and the fruit appears very soft. Serve with whipped cream, crème fraîche or vanilla ice cream.

BARBARA-JO MCINTOSH

Barbara-jo McIntosh is the owner of Vancouver's only bookstore solely dedicated to the world of cookbooks – Barbara-jo's Book to Cooks. Well-known in local culinary circles, Barbara-jo has been involved in the food industry all of her working life – from selling seafood to catering to operating her own restaurant. Since its opening, her unique store, fully equipped with a gas-fired kitchen, has played host to many prominent visiting authors and chefs who are featured at her regular book signing and tasting events. With the publication of her own book, *Tin Fish Gourmet*, Barbara-jo has now joined the impressive rank of cookbook authors represented on her own shelves.

PEACH AND BLUEBERRY COBBLER

The aisles at the Market brim with fresh fruit year round, and nothing is more satisfying than this simple fruit dessert, especially when it follows your brilliant display of pyrotechnics on the barbecue. There are lots of combinations to try: spring rhubarb, apples and quince; apples and blackberries; even plums, apples and huckleberries. Just use what's fresh and available. Be sure to experiment with spices: ground ginger, nutmeg, cinnamon or a hint of cardamom – but one at a time, please!

Preparation time: 45 minutes
Wine pairing: Late-harvest Riesling or Ehrenfelser

Serves 4

2 cups (500 mL) blueberries, washed
2 lbs (900 g) fresh peaches, peeled and sliced
½ tsp (2.5 mL) ground cardamom
1 tsp (5 mL) lemon zest, grated
½ cup (125 mL) Demerara sugar
2 cups plus l tbsp (515 mL) cake flour
1 tbsp (15 mL) baking powder
pinch of salt
⅓ cup (80 mL) cold unsalted butter,
cut into small pieces
¾ cup plus 1 tbsp (200 mL) whipping cream

Oven: 400°F/200°C

1. In a large mixing bowl, combine blueberries and sliced peaches with cardamom, lemon zest, 2 tbsp/30 mL of the sugar and 1 tbsp/15 mL of the cake flour. Toss to mix thoroughly. Transfer the fruit mixture to a deep, ovenproof baking dish or casserole. (In a pinch, a broad Dutch oven will work fine.)
2. In a large bowl, sift together remaining cake flour, baking powder, salt and remaining sugar. Using two dinner knives, combine butter with flour until the mixture resembles coarse meal. Using a rubber spatula, lightly stir in ¾ cup/185 mL of the whipping cream to make a soft and tender dough.
3. Turn the dough out onto a flat surface and roll to ¾ in/2 cm in thickness. With a cookie cutter or glass, cut out 3 in/8 cm rounds. With a steel spatula, arrange the rounds on the fruit and brush with the remaining whipping cream. Bake for 30 to 35 minutes or until the fruit begins to bubble and the pastry rounds are slightly browned.
4. To serve, scoop warm cobbler onto serving plates; top with lightly sweetened whipped cream or vanilla ice cream if desired.

JAMIE MAW

Look up *bon vivant* in the dictionary and you will find a description of Jamie staring back at you. A world traveller, full-time investment banker and full-time food writer (full-time scheduler?), Jamie has his finger firmly on the pulse of fine dining on the world's major continents. Of course, having an office in London comes in handy when it's time to explain the cost of doing lunch in England to Revenue Canada. Being one who believes in living life to its fullest, Jamie loves the Public Market for its celebration of West Coast food and lifestyle. When he's in town and in the mood to entertain, the Market is his favourite place for wild salmon, glistening halibut, ocean-scented shellfish, aged beef and farm-fresh fruits and vegetables.

RHUBARB FOOL

When the first rhubarb of spring appears in the Market, a collective smile appears on the faces of the sun-starved and they sigh, "At last, there's hope." Rhubarb is the harbinger of all the good fruits and berries to come. Even though we think of it as a fruit, it's not – it's a stalk. For Rhubarb Fool there are few ingredients, it's quickly made and it brings any casual dinner to a foolishly pleasant conclusion. The tang of rhubarb varies, as does people's taste for it, so there's a range of sugar in this recipe. Keep in mind that you can always add more sweetness, but it's difficult to take it away. The preserved ginger adds little spicy-sweet bursts of flavour.

Preparation time: 30 minutes
Wine pairing: Late-harvest Riesling or Ehrenfelser

Serves 4

1 lb (450 g) rhubarb
½ to 1 cup (125 to 250 mL) granulated sugar
1 tbsp (15 mL) water
1 cup (250 mL) whipping cream
icing sugar to taste
1 tbsp (15 mL) ginger, finely chopped,
preserved in syrup

RHUBARB

Available from late winter to early summer, only the thick, red, celery-like stems of rhubarb are edible. The leaves contain oxalic acid and are toxic. Pick stalks that are crisp and brightly coloured. Because of its intense tartness, rhubarb is often best sweetened with a generous dose of sugar and used like a fruit in chutneys or sauces, or baked into pies. Rhubarb and strawberries make a great combination.

1. Trim ends from rhubarb stalks and cut stalks crosswise into ½ in/1.25 cm pieces. Place rhubarb, sugar and water in heavy, nonreactive saucepan. Cook over low heat, stirring occasionally, until rhubarb is quite soft, about 15 minutes. (Rhubarb stews beautifully in the microwave oven. Put cut stalks and sugar in large microwave-safe bowl; cover and cook on high until rhubarb is soft, about 5 to 8 minutes in high-powered ovens or up to 12 minutes in smaller ovens. Check for softness as you go.)
2. Transfer stewed rhubarb to a large mixing bowl; let cool. (Rhubarb can be stewed a day in advance.) In a medium bowl, whip cream until stiff peaks form. Add icing sugar to taste. Gently fold whipped cream and chopped ginger into rhubarb. The rhubarb will form bright streaks in the cream. Chill if not serving right away.
3. To serve, spoon into small glass bowls or tall glasses such as martini glasses and serve with small, crisp cookies (see Sugar Spice Cookies, page 222).

MURRAY MCMILLAN

Murray moved – temporarily, he thought – from a "pressure cooker job" as the *Vancouver Sun*'s features editor to overseeing the production of the food pages during a colleague's leave of absence. That was January 1994, and he's been there ever since. "Food has always been a passion. Combining the love of great food and writing in one of North America's finest food cities makes this job great fun," he says. Murray was part of the *Vancouver Sun* team that compiled the best-selling cookbook *Six O'Clock Solutions*. His most recent work is *The New Canadian Basics Cookbook*, the result of a collaboration with cousin Carol Ferguson, food and nutrition editor at *Homemaker's Magazine*.

LEMON VERBENA PANNA COTTA

with Poached Cherries

Panna cotta is an Italian delicacy that literally translates as "clotted cream." Lemon verbena adds a lovely herbal lemon flavour to the panna cotta. A good substitute is the zest of a lemon or lime infused into the cream. The Okanagan Valley grows several outstanding varieties of cherries. For something a little different, try the golden Rainier cherry (with a slightly reddish blush), one of the sweetest cherries available.

Preparation time: 20 minutes (3 hours to set)
Wine pairing: Ehrenfelser or Riesling icewine

Serves 4

Panna Cotta

- 3 cups (750 mL) whipping cream
- 1 cup (250 mL) whole milk
- ½ cup (125 mL) granulated sugar
- 1 vanilla bean, split
- ¼ cup (60 mL) lemon verbena leaves or zest of lemon or lime
- 4 leaves of gelatin or 1 pkg granular gelatin
- 4 small ramekin moulds or custard cups

Cherries

- 1 cup (250 mL) red wine
- ⅓ cup (80 mL) granulated sugar
- 2 cups (500 mL) cherries, pitted
- juice and zest of ½ lemon
- juice and zest of ½ lime
- lemon verbena sprigs for garnish

1. In a large saucepan over medium-high heat, combine the whipping cream, milk and sugar. Stir until sugar is dissolved. Scrape the seeds from the vanilla bean and add, along with the lemon verbena. Bring to a boil and remove immediately from heat.
2. In a stainless steel bowl, soak the gelatin in 1 cup/250 mL cold water until soft. Drain and squeeze out excess moisture. Hold the bowl over a hot burner until the gelatin melts, about 1 minute. Pour the liquid gelatin into the cream mixture and stir well to blend. (If using granular gelatin, simply sprinkle package contents into the hot liquid and stir until dissolved.) Strain into 4 small ramekin moulds or custard dishes and place in refrigerator when cool. Allow to set at least 3 hours.
3. In a medium saucepan over medium-high heat, combine red wine and sugar. Bring to a boil, reduce heat and add cherries. Remove from heat and season with lemon and lime juice and zest. To serve, unmould panna cotta onto plates. Spoon the cherries and poaching liquid around the plate and garnish with sprigs of lemon verbena.

BAILEY'S MOCHA CUSTARD

Edward uses whole coffee beans to infuse the broth with an intense coffee flavour that is balanced by a rich custard and the smooth taste of Bailey's Irish Cream. For a whimsical effect, bake the custard in teacups or simply bake in shallow custard cups. When cool, you can coat the top with granulated sugar and caramelize with a blowtorch or broiler.

Preparation time: 60 minutes
Wine pairing: Riesling or Vidal icewine

Serves 6 to 8

2 cups (500 mL) whipping cream
2 cups (500 mL) whole milk
½ cup (125 mL) espresso coffee beans
2 whole vanilla beans
½ cup (125 mL) dark chocolate, grated
4 large eggs
4 large egg yolks
½ cup (125 mL) granulated sugar
½ cup (125 mL) brown sugar
¼ cup (60 mL) Bailey's Irish Cream
boiling water
sponge candy, finely chopped, for garnish (optional)

Oven: 300°F/150°C

1. In a large, heavy-bottomed saucepan, combine the cream, milk and coffee beans. Cut the vanilla beans in half and scrape the seeds into the pan. Bring to a boil, watching carefully, as the cream will triple in volume and can easily spill over the pan. Remove from heat and stir in the grated chocolate until melted and smooth.
2. In a large bowl, combine the eggs, yolks, granulated sugar and brown sugar. Whisk vigorously until mixture is pale yellow and fluffy. Strain the warm cream mixture into the yolks and stir gently to mix. Add the Bailey's and stir to mix well.
3. Transfer the custard into small coffee or teacups and place them in a large, deep-sided roasting pan. Pour boiling water in the bottom of pan until the water level reaches halfway up the side of the cups. Cover with aluminum foil and bake for 45 minutes or until the custard is set. (A toothpick should come out clean when inserted into the custard.)
4. Transfer to a cooling rack and allow to cool to room temperature. Place in the refrigerator until well chilled and serve with chopped sponge toffee sprinkled on top as a garnish.

COFFEE

One of the most important cash crops in the world, coffee is grown and consumed in many parts of the globe. Each country has a different combination of environmental and plant selection that produces a uniquely flavoured coffee. The art of the roaster is to take these diverse beans and find the appropriate way to roast and blend them to make a harmonious cup of coffee. The darker roasts allow the full, deep flavour of coffee to come forward; overroasting will produce a full flavour but leave a burnt or bitter taste on the palate. In general, light- and medium-roasted beans produce a subtle, elegant coffee that produces nutty and fragrant beverages. Decaffeinated coffee is generally roasted a little more than normal coffee to compensate for the flavour lost during the decaffeination process (the best is Swiss water processed).

SUGAR SPICE COOKIES

These cookies are addictive! Be careful not to lock yourself alone in a room with them. If you use shortening, the cookie will be crisp on the outside and chewy on the inside. Butter will make a crisper cookie with a rich texture.

Preparation time: 45 minutes
Wine pairing: Late-harvest Ehrenfelser or Optima

Makes 24

¾ cup (185 mL) shortening or butter
1 cup (250 mL) brown sugar
1 large egg, lightly beaten
¼ (60 mL) cup molasses
2 cups (500 mL) all-purpose flour
2 tsp (10 mL) baking soda
1 tsp (5 mL) cinnamon
1 tsp (5 mL) ground ginger
½ tsp (2.5 mL) ground cloves
granulated sugar for dipping

Oven: 350°F/180°C

1. In a large bowl, cream the shortening with the brown sugar until the mixture is light and fluffy. Beat in the egg and molasses. In a medium bowl, sift together the flour, baking soda, cinnamon, ginger and cloves.
2. Add the flour mixture in batches to the shortening mixture until well mixed. Cover with plastic wrap and chill the dough for 30 minutes.
3. Roll the dough into small balls and dip one side in the granulated sugar. Arrange the balls, sugar-side up, on a cookie sheet lined with parchment paper. Bake for 10 minutes or until the cookies are puffed and cracked on top. Transfer to a cooling rack. When cool, store in an airtight container. These cookies go well with Rhubarb Fool (see page 216).

HOLLY RODGERS AND DOUG GRAF

Holly and Doug have an enduring passion for the coffee business. After the pair graduated from the University of Victoria, they went on to help Doug's father, Pat, build a thriving business known as The Coffee Roaster. The team was a fixture at the Granville Island store, roasting fresh coffee before the eyes of appreciative clients. After the sale of the business, Doug became a consultant for the fairly traded coffee program of a local international development agency. The program was dear to Doug's heart, as it helped foster the awareness of organic agriculture and human rights in coffee-growing countries. In the spring of 1999 the couple returned to the Market and opened Origins Coffee, which, true to their convictions, sells only organic and fairly traded coffee. The couple's store has attracted considerable attention for its elegant design and for filling a void in a city where organic coffee is still a rare find. Doug spends part of each day roasting prime beans in an antique French roaster, then blending the coffee to perfection.

COOKING TEMPERATURE CHART
(using an instant-read meat thermometer)

Meat Cut or Product		°F	°C
Beef/Veal and Lamb: roasts, steaks and chops	RARE	145	63
Beef/Veal and Lamb: roasts, steaks and chops	MEDIUM	160	71
Beef/Veal and Lamb: roasts, steaks and chops	WELL DONE	170	77
Pork: roasts, steaks and chops	MEDIUM	160	71
Pork: roasts, steaks and chops	WELL DONE	170	77
Pork: whole ham (cook before serving)		160	71
Ground Beef/Veal, Lamb, Pork, Chicken or Turkey	SAFETY MINIMUM	160	71
Chicken or Turkey: whole (test thigh – juices should run clear)		180	82
Chicken or Turkey: breast only		170	77
Chicken or Turkey: stuffing		165	74

glossary of cooking terms

GLOSSARY OF COOKING TERMS

Blanching

Blanching is simply partially cooking by boiling in salted water. A light blanching is best to preserve the vitamin content of vegetables and to cook until them until they are tender but still crisp. Blanching is used to prepare ingredients such as asparagus and green beans in advance and, in the case of green vegetables, to set the colour. Vegetables are often blanched and then plunged into ice water to stop the cooking process and to quickly cool them.

Braising

Braising is slow cooking, usually in an aromatic liquid. It is useful in rendering tough cuts of meat meltingly tender. Braising in oil is a technique known as confit. Bring the liquid to a simmer and transfer to a medium oven for up to 2 hours, or to a low oven for up to 4 hours. If the top seems to be browning too quickly, turn the items over and reduce heat or cover with aluminum foil.

Chopping

The finer you can slice or dice a product, the faster the cooking time and the more consistent the end result. Try to keep most ingredients the same approximate size. We recommend a good stainless steel chef's knife for most applications. Inexpensive Chinese or Japanese vegetable cleavers also work very well. (Make sure you buy a stainless steel model, if available.) Use a good plastic cutting board if possible. Wood boards are a good second choice but require thorough cleaning; use distilled vinegar or lemon and salt to freshen and disinfect.

Deep-frying

For deep-frying, the oil must be hot to avoid excess fat from soaking into the batter.
The oil should be at least 350°F/180°C for most applications. The oil will bubble rapidly around a wooden chopstick when the correct temperature is reached. Always drain the product on paper towels to remove surface grease. If the oil is heated too high it may burst into flames. If that happens, cover with a lid to smother the flames. Having a fire extinguisher nearby is a smart idea in all kitchens.

Pan-frying

Pan-frying is cooking in a skillet or frying in a little more oil than is needed for stir-frying. Pan-frying is done over medium heat until a thin brown crust has formed. Whatever is being fried is then flipped and the second side is cooked until golden brown. Be sure to cook meat thoroughly. Chicken or other meat can be transferred to a hot oven to finish the cooking.

Roasting

Roasting is a wonderful way to enhance the flavour of vegetables, meats or seafood. The oven is usually at a high temperature (400°F/200°C), and what is being roasted is often coated with a light film of oil (which promotes browning and crisping). Food with a high sugar content, such as yams or pumpkin, will brown more quickly. A little charring is often a nice complement to the sweet inner flesh.

Steaming

Steaming can be utilized to quickly cook food while retaining flavour and texture. The ingredients can be placed over boiling water or aromatic cooking liquid, covered and left to steam until cooked through. You can buy a steamer consisting of a pot bottom, two layers of metal steaming trays and a domed lid. A simpler solution is to set a grid or rack in the bottom of a wok with a large lid on top. If you don't have a rack, chopsticks, bowls or spare wok rings on the bottom of the wok all make excellent platforms for steaming.

Stir-frying

Stir-frying is the quick cooking of food by tossing it in a hot wok or frying pan. Usually a little oil and aromatic seasonings like garlic or ginger are used to flavour the oil. If the ingredients are cooking too quickly, lower the heat or add a little liquid to prevent vegetables from scorching.

Toasting (nuts and seeds)

Place the nuts or seeds in a dry fry pan over medium heat. Constantly stir and toss the pan until the contents begin to brown. Be careful not to burn the contents. When the nuts or seeds are golden, remove from pan quickly and transfer to a plate to cool. The same procedure can be performed using a baking tray in a moderate (350°F/180°C) oven. Bake until the nuts are warmed through and just beginning to brown.

GRANVILLE ISLAND PUBLIC MARKET MERCHANT DIRECTORY

Merchant		Telephone (604)	P.O. Box
31	A La Mode	685-8335	137
28	Armando's Finest Quality Meats	685-0359	149
13	Babushka's Kitchen	669-4119	150
8	Blue Parrot Espresso Bar	688-5127	108
3	Buddy's Farm	684-6801	105
44	Candy Kitchen	681-7001	142
9	Celine's Fish & Chips	669-8650	109
20	Dressed To Go Poultry	682-5811	126
22	Duso's Pasta & Cheese	685-5921	120
43	Dussa's Ham & Cheese	688-8881	144
24	Four Seasons Farm	682-2215	121
14	Fraser Valley Juice & Salad Bar	669-0727	113
37	Gaia Garden Herbal Dispensary	689-4372	127
6	Gourmet Wok	688-5581	106
39	The Grainry	681-6426	129
15	Gran Isle Turkey Stop	681-4543	132
47	Granville Island Florist	669-1228	124
17	Granville Island Poultryland	669-5457	N/A
26	Granville Island Produce	662-3048	135
35	Granville Island Tea Company	683-7491	130
23	House of Brussels Chocolates	684-9678	136
46	JJ Bean – The Coffee Roaster	685-0613	138
2	Kaisereck Deli	685-8810	114
5	La Tortilleria	684-8220	145
34	Laurelle's Fine Foods	685-8482	148
45	Lee's Donuts	685-4021	122
1	Longliner Sea Foods	681-9016	102
30	Market Grill	689-1918	104
42	The Milkman	687-7597	139
7	Muffin Granny	684-3821	115
32	Okanagan Wine Shops	684-3364	146
27	Olde World Fudge	687-7355	133
10	Omi of Japan	685-8011	110
16	Origins Coffee	684-5552	103
11	Phoenix Fast Food	684-1714	111
12	Pizza Pzzaz	689-9002	131

29	Post Office/Lotto	682-5495	140
18	Salmon Shop	669-3474	112
49	Seafood City	688-1818	143
25	Siegel's Bagels	685-5670	134
21	The Smoke Shop	669-9223	119
36	South China Seas Trading Co.	681-5402	125
33	Stock Market	687-2433	147
40	Stuart's Bakery	685-8816	123
48	Sunlight Farms	684-0830	101
41	Tenderland Meats	688-6951	141
4	Terra Breads	685-3102	107
19	V & J Plant Shop	689-4439	116
38	Zara's Pasta Nest	683-2935	128

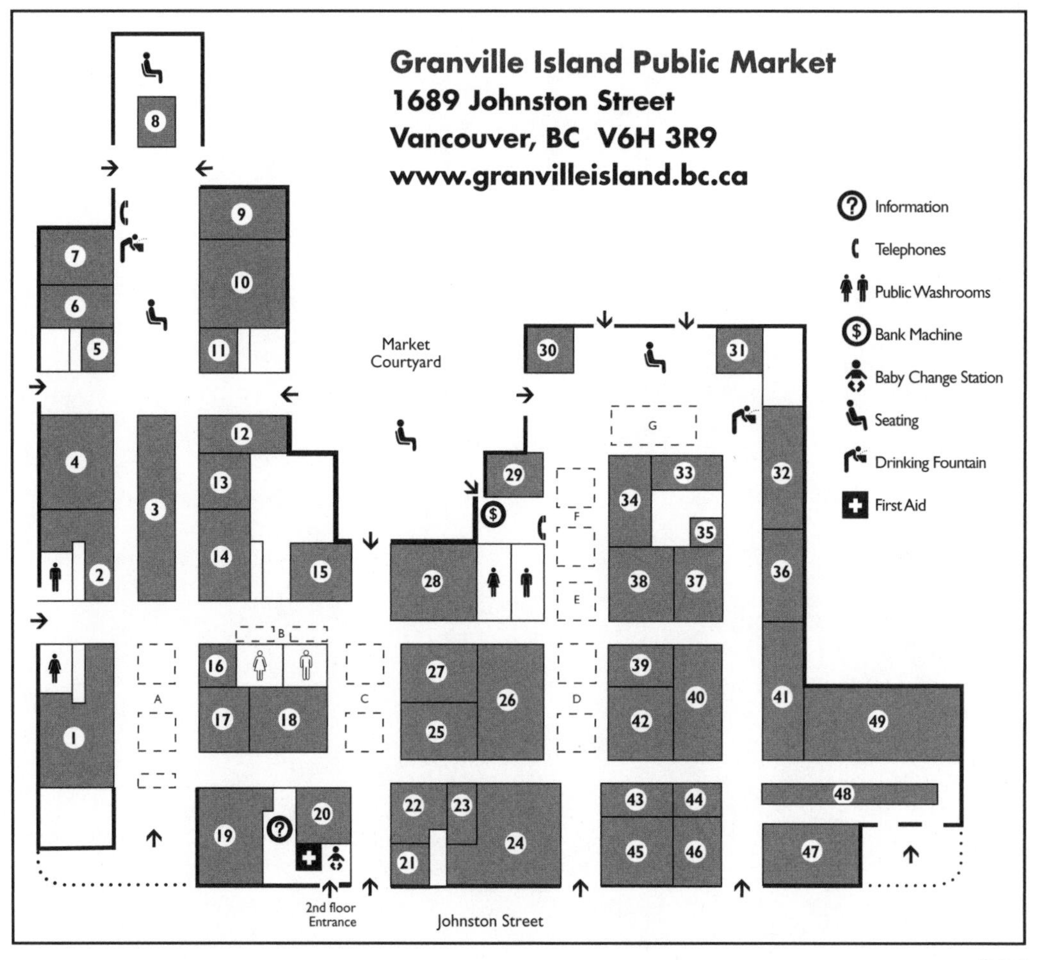

index

BILL JONES

Co-host of *Chefs in the Market* with Stephen Wong, Bill has a long and distinguished background in the food and wine industry. His chef training began at the feet of his father (an excellent cook), who instilled in Bill a love of good ingredients and a passion for making people happy through great food. Formal training at the prestigious L'École de Cuisine Français, under Sabine de Mirbeck, led to stints in England and France working with great chefs such as Antoine Mosimann, Anthony Worrel-Thompson and Jean-Paul Bossée.

Locally, Bill has worked in many fine kitchens, including Sooke Harbour House, Dufour & Co. and the Raintree. For the past four years, he has built up his consulting company, Magnetic North Cuisine, into a diverse force in the food and wine fields. His projects range from book and recipe development to restaurant management and marketing. Bill is a frequent teacher at local cooking schools and is particularly known for his expertise in mushrooms and wild foods. *Chefs in the Market* is his fifth book to date, and third – along with *New World Noodles* and *New World Chinese Cooking* (Robert Rose 1997, 1998) – co-written with Stephen Wong. His most recent book is an ode to garden-fresh food, *Sublime Vegetarian* (Douglas & McIntyre, 1999).

STEPHEN WONG

Chefs in the Market co-host Stephen Wong developed a love for fine food early in life. He recalls fondly his Sunday excursions as a child to the wet markets in Hong Kong with his amah, where he poked and prodded through the piles of produce, learning how to select the best ingredients for their family dinners. After working in some of the best award-winning dining rooms in B.C., such as Le Gavroche, Sooke Harbour House and the Raintree, and owning and operating two restaurants, Cherrystone Cove and Cheyna, he decided to venture into food writing.

As a food and wine journalist, Wong has contributed to books, magazines and newspapers both nationally and internationally. He is also the author or co-author of three cookbooks: *HeartSmart Chinese Cooking*, commissioned by the Heart and Stroke Foundation (Douglas & McIntyre, 1996), *New World Noodles* and *New World Chinese Cooking* (Robert Rose, 1997, 1998), both co-written with Bill Jones. In addition, Wong has been travelling to Pacific Rim countries such as China and Japan on food trade missions, representing Canadian trade agencies and private-sector food exporters.